Developing
Healthy Churches

Robert Warren

CHURCH HOUSE
PUBLISHING

Church House Publishing
Church House
Great Smith Street
London SW1P 3AZ

Emails: copyright@c-of-e.org.uk

The opinions expressed in this book are those of the authors and do not
necessarily reflect the official policy of the General Synod or
The Archbishops' Council of The Church of England

ISBN 978 0 7151 4281 3

Typeset by Regent Typesetting, London
Printed and bound by
CPI Group (UK) Ltd, Croydon CR0 4YY

Contents

Marks of a healthy church

as defined and described in

The Healthy Churches' Handbook

A healthy church:

- is energized by faith
- has an outward-looking focus
- seeks to find out what God wants
- faces the cost of change and growth
- operates as a community
- makes room for all
- does a few things and does them well.

Introduction

The Healthy Churches' Handbook, published in 2004, has been widely used across churches in the UK and beyond. That book was the fruit of listening to the stories of 25 churches in the Durham diocese which had grown over the previous five years. From listening to their stories, seven marks emerged of what these churches had in common (see p. iv). Those marks were spelt out and explored in the book. Since then, I have engaged with many churches, in different ways, about the issues raised in that book.

This has involved the leading of over one hundred Healthy Churches Exercises, sometimes with a number of churches meeting together on the same day and doing the exercise in parallel. It has also included working with over fifty churches that have been developing Mission Action Plans (MAPs) and observing churches as they wrestle to discern the call of God on their corporate life. Also, and at greater depth, I have continued to work with a small group of churches as a continuing consultant, usually to the incumbent/minister.

What is meant by a healthy church?

The particular way in which health is understood throughout this book is as a translation of the biblical concept of salvation, namely wholeness, balance and harmony with God and all creation. Christ frequently said to people whom he had healed, 'your faith has saved you'. This is variously translated 'made you well', 'made you whole'. So a healthy church is one that has been touched and energized by the presence of God so that it reflects something of the good news of the wholeness made possible through the knowledge of God as revealed in Christ, by the Holy Spirit.

Out of this experience I have seen plenty of wonderful demonstrations of the marks of a healthy church, usually expressed in ways I could never have imagined. Also, I have seen where, why and how churches wrestle against obstacles to their moving towards greater wholeness as a church.

The Healthy Churches' Handbook offered a range of practical suggestions for moving forward on each of the marks of a healthy church. Yet often I have sensed people saying about those marks – 'Yes, but how?' They do not wish to argue with the seven marks, but they would like help in knowing how to give expression to them. *Developing Healthy Churches* seeks to address that. It does so in several ways.

The Foundations section (Chapters 1–4) explores 'the issues behind the issues'. These include clarifying what church is all about (Chapter 1), identifying where and why churches find progress towards health difficult to achieve (Chapter 2), exploring the resources that the church can draw on to make progress (Chapter 3) and suggesting a structure for making progress towards being a healthy church (Chapter 4).

The Practicalities section (Chapters 5–10) goes on to explore six areas that churches most regularly express a desire to find creative ways of addressing. These are the areas of *spirituality*, *pastoral care*, *home groups*, *giving*, *evangelism* and *mission*. Drawing on the stories of the joys, struggles and creative responses of churches in those areas, the six chapters identify key goals and offer a range of ideas about how to achieve those goals.

The Resources section makes available a number of resources and exercises developed in past years to help churches review specific aspects of their life. It is in two parts. The first part is essentially a study guide, for *personal* or *group* work. The second part contains material to help leaders, leadership groups and anyone with responsibility for shaping the life of the church. Either part can also be used as the basis for a *sermon series*. All this material can be studied the whole way through, but works equally well as an aid to the study and exploration of one issue at a time.

Throughout the book there are other resources as well. There are regular references to the *seven marks* of a healthy church which link back to *The Healthy Churches' Handbook.* Originally I had expected this book to be built around those seven marks. It has not worked out that way, and maybe that is because it does not 'work out like that' in real life. The marks are so woven together 'in the web of life' that they cannot be isolated like that.

In each of the Foundations section chapters there is a box in which the *biblical basis* of the chapter subject can be found. It is important to make this connection between the scriptures and the reality of church life today. May those connections increase.

There are also *instructive stories* scattered throughout the book. It is hoped that these will illuminate the point being made and also assure readers that what is suggested is not idealism, but ideals that have been embedded in the experience of some churches. In this sense *Developing Healthy Churches* continues the approach of *The Healthy Churches' Handbook* in so listening to what the Spirit is saying to the churches, that something of the mind of Christ can be grasped. All that is offered is the fruit of listening to many stories of how churches are developing the *quality* of church life. This book is really the fruit of what many churches are doing and finding, rather than what one person has theorized about.

The first five chapters all end with a *spiritual exercise*. If, as is argued in the first chapter, the heart of church life is our exploration and expression of what it means to know God, then resources to help us encounter God are needed if the church is to fulfil its calling. In the first place these spiritual exercises are intended for personal use. However, they are valuable disciplines to introduce into church life too.

Many have contributed to this book, none more so than my good friend the Revd Canon John Holmes, who led growing churches in inner-city Leeds before becoming Missioner in the Ripon and Leeds diocese and then Canon Missioner in the Wakefield diocese. He continues, in retirement, to make a gracious and generous contribution to the well-being of many churches, and people. He has given detailed attention to the script and made many insightful contributions. The book has been significantly enriched by his thorough reading of my manuscripts. The limitations of this work, however, need to be laid at my feet as John has only contributed to its limitations by limiting their number.

I commend this companion to *The Healthy Churches' Handbook* to all who long to see the Church flourish in the twenty-first century and reflect more fully the likeness of Christ. In the final issue, it is Christ himself who has drawn us to faith in him and called us to be a living demonstration of his compassion for all people.

My prayer is that this work may be of help in enabling the light of Christ to shine more clearly through his Church today.

Robert Warren

Part 1:
Foundations

Chapter 1
What's it all about?

These are challenging days in the life of the Church.

It is called upon to bear witness to 'eternal verities' in a world addicted to what is new, and guided by personally constructed creeds drawn from a mish-mash of philosophies. It is called to 'be still and know that I am God' in a world where everyone is rushing about and fearful of stillness or silence. It is called to be a community in a world focused on the freedom and independence of the individual, indeed where identity is defined over against any community or norms of society. Moreover the Church, that has for so long been at the centre of society and government, and has become used to its role at the centre of power, now finds itself marginalized and, at least relatively, powerless.

The word *parochial* says it all. We understand it to point to what is local, predictable, normal and safe. Above all it points to a sense of rootedness and belonging. Yet the word comes from Peter's description of the churches to which he wrote, and, translated literally, means 'aliens', or rather, 'resident aliens': the odd ones, the misfits. As the epistle to Diognetus, written in AD 150 puts it:

> They live in countries of their own, but simply as sojourners;
> they share the life of citizens, they endure the lot of foreigners;
> every foreign land is to them a fatherland, and every fatherland
> a foreign land.[1]

In such challenging circumstances it is hardly surprising that many churches are in decline numerically and ageing in the process. The older generation is not being replaced.[2] Declining church incomes are a headache for many, sucking some churches in a fund-raising spiral which ends up consuming virtually all the church's energies and attention. While all this is happening, clergy numbers are in decline, with 41 per cent of stipendiary clergy and 60 per cent of all currently serving clergy due to retire by 2020.

But it is not just the statistics. In many ways the culture is against us. Our Christian heritage seems like a steadily retreating tide. The Christian ethical framework plays a decreasing part in shaping much of the contemporary moral climate. Things are not looking good.

Yet the tide is not all one way. Some churches, indeed dioceses, are seeing growth. People continue to come to faith, and many personal stories on *Songs of Praise* are remarkable ones of faith being lived out in testing circumstances and people experiencing the reality of God in the darkest of settings. Good news happens.

That happening of the good news of Jesus Christ comes, very often, through the Church; whether in the sense of the Church itself doing things that help people come to faith, or people finding in Christians (who are the Church) the way to God and to finding meaning and purpose in life.

Like a small boat caught in the midst of strong cross-currents, the Church needs to know where it is going. It also needs to hold fast to that ultimate vision, however much it feels pulled in different directions. It may take all our energies to navigate our way through these currents, so it is vital that limited energies are used well.

The heart of the matter

The management guru Tom Peters advises businesses, when facing adverse trading conditions, to 'stick to the knitting'; that is, to focus on their core business. The Church today needs to be clear about *its* core business and avoid getting distracted into other matters, however attractive and enticing.

> **The first mark of a healthy church:**
>
> it is **energized by faith**

Although the Church is not a business, we can sharpen our perception if we use familiar marketing terminology to identify what we are about. So what is the *Church's core business*? The central thesis of this book is that the 'product' which the Church is called to 'market' is nothing other than *the knowledge of God*. 'Knowledge' is meant here in its primary sense of knowing someone rather than gathering information.

As John Baillie, the Scottish theologian, put it many years ago, in the opening sentence of his book, *Our Knowledge of God*:

> The great fact for which all religion stands is the confrontation of the human soul with the transcendent holiness of God.[3]

Biblical roots

The whole of scripture is the story of people who encountered God and for whom that meeting permanently transformed who they were and what they did.

Abraham: the senior citizen becomes Abraham the pilgrim as he responds to God's call to go to the land God would show him. Abraham and Sarah, the childless senior citizens, became the parents of a vast people. The whole story unfolds in terms of their many encounters with God.

Moses: the bulrushes-baby and palace-misfit finds his vocation at a burning bush in the desert while in enforced early retirement. There he meets with God and not only leads the children of Israel across the Red Sea, but teaches the whole world, through the Ten Commandments, an ethical framework for living and for society that has never been surpassed.

Jesus: proclaimed at his birth as Son of God, encounters God in his baptism as the one who defines him in terms of his relationship with God: 'You are my Son, the Beloved' after which he devotes his life to pursuing that relationship and passing it on to the new Israel he brings into being.

Paul: knocked off his horse by the presence of God and off his high horse of prejudice against Jesus Christ, goes on to live his life in response to the call of God at every turn, laying the foundations of the faith and the Church as he does so.

Scripture is the record of people encountering the holiness of God.

Classic texts: The many Gospel encounters with Jesus (e.g. Bartimaeus **Mark 10.46–52**); **Hebrews 13.**

Albert Einstein was feeling his way after this knowledge when he wrote:

> The most beautiful experience we can have is the mysterious. It is the fundamental emotion that stands at the cradle of true art and true science. Whoever does not know it and can no longer wonder, no longer marvel, is as good as dead, and his eyes are dimmed. It was the experience of mystery – even if mixed with fear – that engendered religion. A knowledge of the existence

of something we cannot penetrate, our perceptions of the profoundest reason and the most radiant beauty, which only in their most primitive forms are accessible to our minds: it is this knowledge and this emotion that constitute true religiosity. In this sense, and only this sense, I am a deeply religious man … I am satisfied with the mystery of life's eternity and with a knowledge, a sense, of the marvellous structure of existence – as well as the humble attempt to understand even a tiny portion of the Reason that manifests itself in nature.[4]

This is what the Church, with limited resources, needs to devote its energies and attention and best endeavours to today. This is always how the Church finds the renewal of its life and vitality. The New Testament church, the monastic movement, the Celtic saints and church, the Reformation, the Evangelical Revival, the Oxford Movement and Charismatic Renewal, to name but a few, are all examples of what happens when the pursuit of the knowledge of God moves centre stage in the life of the Church. As Bishop Alan Smith puts it:

The focus of all that we are and all that we do is God. It is not, in the first instance, church – or even mission. When other things become our main focus we will be little more than a campaigning group … a heritage lobby, a self-help group catering for the needs of its members, or simply an outdated organization looking beyond its membership to delay the arrival of its sell-by date.[5]

This knowledge of God can be seen as operating in three intertwined dimensions, illustrated in the diagram on page 7.

This is the heart of the Christian faith, this is what it is all about, knowing God. Yet in the busy-ness of church life it is all too easy to miss it. The 'heart' in scripture is the seat of our relating to God. So the need of the hour is for individuals to return to the heart of what the faith is all about: our pursuit of the knowledge of God and its outworking in our lives. For that to happen, the Church needs equally to have this focus in its life, nurturing and giving expression to its faith in God in all that it does.

This return to the heart of what Church is all about needs to find expression within all three of these dimensions.[6]

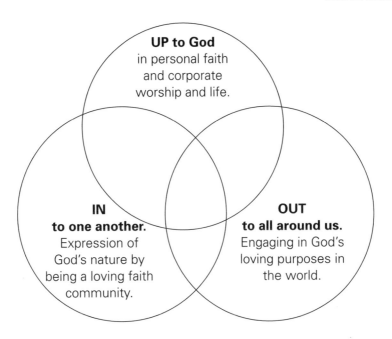

Knowing God today

The knowledge of God begins in personal and corporate relationship with God.

This finds expression in the way the Church focuses its pastoral work of helping people begin the journey of faith in God as well as in helping those already on that journey to encounter God particularly at the crossroads of decision-making in their lives. It is given particular expression in public worship which needs, quite consciously, to be conducted with the aim of helping people, individually and corporately, to encounter God. It involves helping people to see their life's story in the light of the greater story of God's revelation in Christ. Leaders of worship need to be sure that this is what they are doing in fulfilling their role in services. Equally, all participants need to come with this same purpose in mind. This encounter with God informs and shapes our lives, shaping us around the grace, goodness and generosity of God as seen in the life of Christ.

This first dimension of Christian and church life, namely the knowledge of God, bears witness to the spiritual dimension of life lacking in our secular world. In the very act of paying attention to God, the Church, thereby, has something to offer to the world.[7]

Sharing in God's life today

Second, we give expression to the knowledge of God by the way that we are Church. As John Wesley put it, 'there is no such thing as solitary religion'. So when it comes to the life of the Church and our part in it, we need to recognize that we are called to play our part, with fellow believers, in giving expression to the image of God revealed in the life of Christ. How relationships are handled, and the values that operate in the Church, are part of our worship; as is the way the Church manages and expresses its life.[8] In today's society the way the Church *is* the Church is a profound way of worshipping God and making known the good news of Christ. 'See how these Christians love one another' remains a key means of 'making Christ known'.

This should be evident in the quality of relationships, in the ability to listen to one another, the way conflicts are handled, and the courage and generosity to create a diverse community that spans age, social, ethnic and educational barriers and celebrates and makes room for diversity.

The Church is called to live now the life of the world to come. The words at the administration of Communion ('The body/blood of Christ keep you in eternal life') remind us of this calling. Eternal life is not simply about life going on for ever after death. Eternal life is about a new quality of life, here and now, not a bigger quantity of life in the future. 'Eternal life' means literally 'the life of the Age to Come'. That life has broken in already through the life of Christ. The believer is called to enter into it, and live by its values, in the here and now. The Church's corporate calling is to give physical expression to this new age; to incarnate the truth of God in a human community living by a different set of values. In the Eucharist we receive the grace of God afresh to fulfil this calling in our day and setting.[9]

Joining in with God's purposes today

The third dimension of the Church's fundamental call, namely, to pursue the knowledge of God, is expressed through our engaging in God's purposes in the world. Those purposes are purposes of love for all creation, bringing it to the fulfilment of its nature and purpose. It finds

> **The third mark of a healthy church:**
>
> it ***seeks to find out what God wants.***

expression both personally (in daily living) and corporately (by the way the Church operates). This also involves setting creation (which includes the natural order and the human dimension) free from oppressive and seductive forces that draw them away from those loving purposes. In this calling the Church needs to work with all seeking the good of the present world as well as to witness to God's valuing of all people and his plan to draw out his image in all. While sharing this loving concern for the world around us, classically expressed in caring for the needy, the Church yet has something distinctive to say. It is about God's valuing of all and his purposes of love for all people and, indeed, all creation.

It has been well argued that a major reason for the spread of Christianity in the early centuries after Christ was because a new purpose for life had come into being.[10] The Greek gods were a frighteningly unpredictable and immoral lot. The Roman gods were characterized by fatalism and human powerlessness to do anything about 'the fates'. By contrast, the Church proclaimed, and demonstrated, that 'God is working his purposes out as year succeeds to year'. This purposeful vision finds expression in the Lord's Prayer that God's kingdom may come and his will be done. To pray this prayer, rightly understood, is to devote our energies to the coming of that new order.

> The years AD 250–253 were tough years for the Christians in Carthage. They began with one of the most vicious outbreaks of persecution, torture and death in the Decian persecutions. No sooner had that come to an end than their city was struck by a plague (thought to have been measles). The church was faced with a tough decision, do they get out while they can, as many of the wealthier citizens were doing, so that the church would survive beyond this plague, or should they stay to care for the sick and dying and risk not only their lives but the very existence of the church in the future? Bishop Cyprian urged the church to stay and care, which is what they did. Despite being those who spent most time nursing the sick and burying the dead, the death rate in the church was noticeably lower than in the wider population. When the plague had passed, many in the local community, including some of their former persecutors, flocked to join the church because they wanted to be part of its purposeful living, seeking the well-being of others and the world in which they lived.[11]

Too easily the Church today fails to grasp the scope of its calling in this dimension of its life. In times of struggle and difficulty it is so tempting to draw resources into church life rather than turn out in loving concern for the wider world.

In practice

In practice these three dimensions of the knowledge of God are not sealed units. The reality of life is that there is constant interplay and interweaving of the three elements. However, it is of real value to see these different elements and their comparative strengths (or weaknesses) in our lives. Doing so points us to where God is calling us to move on.

This framework also helps us to understand the journey that we, and others whom we are seeking to help, may be on. Perhaps the normal pattern is that people come into a relationship with God ('Up') that causes them to become involved in the life of a church ('In') and, in due course, to be involved in some form of service ('Out'). However, there are many other ways in which people enter into and journey through these aspects of the knowledge of God.

> David described himself as an atheist, but he was very supportive of his wife's involvement in the church. As an electrician he was always ready to help the church if there was some crisis that needed his skills. Through that involvement he struck up friendships with a number of men in the church. At one point the church was involved in a mission and asked him to come along to help with the practical work of setting up their equipment. Through involvement in that project he came to personal faith. 'Service–friendship–faith', 'Out'–'In'–'Up' was the map of his journey.

> Lucy was not a churchgoer but she got on really well with several of the leaders of the Parent and Toddler group she attended regularly. She was then diagnosed as having cancer and turned to those friends 'from the church'. Their loving support was a major factor in helping her through surgery and back to health, but it was their faith that deeply affected her. By the time she was on the road to recovery she knew herself to be loved by God. Once she had recovered, she joined the Parent and Toddler group leaders. Only later on did she start going to church. 'Friendship–faith–service–church', or 'In'–'Up'–'Out'–'In' described her journey.

This framework is not a rigid framework or system into which everyone should be squeezed. Rather it is a map of the territory that churches need to be familiar with. Bearing it in mind, personally and corporately, enables us to know what is going on, and where our efforts (including prayer) need to be focused.

Return to the heart

Tough though it is in practice, the task of the Church is really quite simple.

Our calling is to nurture a loving relationship to God, to one another within the Church and to the world around. It certainly calls for faith, sacrifice and 'sheer dogged endurance', yet it constitutes a clear and straightforward agenda for the Church expressed in the three dimensions of 'Up' to God, 'In' to one another and 'Out' to the world. Such an agenda constitutes a recall to the heart of God's revelation in Jesus Christ and its outworking in the life of the Church today.

Because these three dimensions describe the whole call of the Church, each of the seven marks of a healthy church outlined in *The Healthy Churches' Handbook*,[12] will find expression in a church that is seeking to return to the heart of what Church is all about. However, three of those marks are particularly crucial for churches seeking the return to the heart of what it is all about.

The first mark, *energized by faith*, describes churches where spirituality is sufficiently nurtured as to be at the heart of the church's life. The third mark, *seeks to find out what God wants*, describes a church where the nurturing of faith is not just at the personal level but shapes the way in which the church operates. In such churches spirituality has invaded their decision-making processes. The seventh mark, *does a few things and does them well*, describes a church that is at peace because it has 'returned to the heart' of what the faith is all about. Such churches are focused rather than frantic. Moreover, it is in churches that are not overwhelmed by activity and programmes that there is enough space for proper reflection on its life and the things that matter most to take place.

These three dimensions, then – looking *up* to God, *in* towards one another, and *out* to the world around – give shape to the Church's calling to be in the business of exploring, expressing and passing on to others our core message, that God can be known. It is in pursuit of these priorities that the health and fruitfulness of the Church in any setting is most likely to be in evidence.

In another key

Another way of expressing the heart of the Church's life, as giving expression to the knowledge of God, is to transpose it into the key of the *love of God.* The scriptures describe love as not just something that God *does*, but, as the very nature of God: God *is* love.

To pursue the knowledge of God is to pursue the love of God. This is best 'read' in the double sense of seeking both to engage with *God's love for us* and all creation and also seeking to give expression to *our love for God* and others. The two great commandments make it clear that love for God and love for others are two sides of the one coin. We cannot choose one over the other. They are only valid when held and expressed together.

In working through and living out the implications of all that this book is about, churches, and – in particular – church leaders, may well wish to speak in terms of the love of God as 'what it is all about'. That is best done as a conscious choice that is consistently held to throughout the application of all that follows.

In people

Having argued that the purpose of the Church is the pursuit and expression of the knowledge of God, there is one vital qualification that needs to be added. Because Christianity is an incarnate faith, this pursuit of the knowledge of God needs to be looked for, and given expression in *people* and in *communities of faith.*

Where the knowledge of God can be seen is in people making the journey into wholeness as people and in churches that are healthy, life-giving, communities. In a previous book[13] I proposed that one of the ways in which the gospel of Christ can be described for today's culture is that:

> God's way of being fully human
> has been demonstrated in the life of Jesus Christ,
> is available to all by work of the Holy Spirit,
> and is currently being demonstrated
> in your nearest local church.

To which the obvious question is – but, is it? At best it is imperfectly so; nonetheless this reminds us that the evidence of the gospel should be found in the lives of individuals and communities who follow the way of Christ so fully that something of the likeness and nature of Christ can be seen in them.

Connecting with God 1: *Stilling*

David Runcorn argues that the best road to the growth of the Church is along the pathway of spiritual growth.[14] Complementary to that, this book argues that the way to grow the Church is to facilitate the growth of people. A vital way to bring about the growth of people, their growth in faith and their knowledge of God, is by introducing them to simple patterns of prayer and meditation. In the first five chapters of this book a spiritual exercise is offered (numbered for ease of reference). Making this regularly part of personal, and then corporate, practice is one of the best ways of enabling a whole faith community to return to the heart of the faith, namely our knowing God.

In our frantic culture, stillness is hard to come by. One way of slowing down is to follow this simple pattern. It can be done in a minute or two (omitting the candle and suggested movements), but is best done as a regular habit and giving it more time (starting, say, with ten minutes, then letting that time expand as we wish and as we have opportunity). It is a great way to start a meeting, but practise it personally first so that it is a natural part of how *you* connect with God.

- *Light a candle* as a sign of God's presence and his ability to transform every situation just as sunlight lights up any location.[15]

- *Be still* – for at least 30 seconds.

- *Give thanks* – wordlessly – for the gift of life: let your mind highlight specific aspects of life you lift to God with thanksgiving, such as your body, your 'nearest and dearest', creation, human creativity, material resources, the wonder of it all. Do not say words: just hold thoughts as thanksgivings to God.

- *Let go* of all that troubles you and weighs you down. It helps to do this by sitting comfortably, with your hands facing down on your thighs. Name what you want to let go, into the loving hands of God, and see your hands releasing your grip on this worry. In doing so you let go its hold on you.

■ *Receive from God* his presence, grace and goodness. Here it helps to turn your hands up, still resting on your thighs, and to name those gifts of God you wish to receive. St Augustine said, 'God gives where he finds open hands.' So receive, naming them before God, such gifts as God's mercy, wisdom, strength, forgiveness, courage, etc. It is best to use single words, or – at most – a phrase.

In such ways we can practise the presence of God and reconnect with what Church and the faith are all about. It is important to do that for its own sake, but also because there is so much to distract us from connecting with God. Which is why we turn now to face head-on the obstacles to the pursuit of the knowledge of God in the life of the Church today.

For further help see *Part 3: Resources*, 'Introduction', pp. 137–9 and, 'Study questions', pp. 140–2.

Chapter 2
Overcoming obstacles

If the task of the Church is to pursue and give incarnated expression, individually and corporately, to the knowledge of God, why is that not more widely evident? What is blocking the journey of churches into expressing more fully the marks of a healthy church? Many clergy and lay people long for the Church to be a vibrant centre of Christian spirituality and life, so why does the Church give another impression?

> Fewer and fewer persons are attracted to Christianity in the 'First World' countries because there is so little spirituality in religion.[1]

> It is disturbing and revealing to hear that the criticism of the church by spiritual seekers outside it is no longer that it is 'boring', 'out of date' or 'irrelevant'. It is criticized instead for being 'unspiritual'.[2]

One of the first things to acknowledge is that every church, every faith community, is unique, just as each of us is unique. This means that no simple 'catch all' can span the sheer diversity of causes that block the expression of spiritual vitality in our churches. However, there are common themes, even if they work themselves out in different ways between one church and another.

We turn now to consider some key obstacles, and what it might take to overcome them.

Biblical roots to overcoming obstacles

Scripture is not only the story of people who encounter the transcendent holiness of God, but also the story of the many obstacles they encounter on their life journey of following God.

Adam and Eve falling at the first hurdle, the children of Israel longing for the 'flesh pots of Egypt', Elijah hounded into the wilderness by Jezebel, sensitive Jeremiah dumped in a well, Daniel and his friends in a lion's den, Jacob wrestling with God as he makes a fearful return to the brother he cheated, Moses facing the lack of food and water in the wilderness, Nehemiah overcoming physical attack and psychological warfare in the rebuilding of Jerusalem; all are symptomatic of a people having to battle for survival.

No wonder Jesus, experiencing the same opposition from religious leaders and the political powers that led eventually to his brutal torture and crucifixion, taught his followers to expect the same battles: 'so persecuted they the prophets who were before you' (Matthew 5.12). Supremely in his passion, Jesus overcame the oppressive power of Roman and religious leaders through sacrificial love and 'opened the kingdom of heaven to all believers'.

No wonder, either, that the last book of the Bible coins a new term for the believer: those who overcome. Perhaps the greatest wonder is that Jesus did what Paul taught, that in a profoundly counter-intuitive way, the believer is called to overcome evil with good.

Classic texts: Matthew 5.38–42; Mark 3.1–6; Luke 4.1–13; Romans 12; 1 Corinthians 13.

The tyranny of the urgent

The sheer busy-ness of life and the endless list of tasks that need to be done, prevent clergy and laity alike from engaging with the things that really matter. Faced with a choice between addressing what is *urgent* and what is *important*, most of us, honestly, go for the urgent, simply because it shouts louder and promises more immediate returns. In doing so we fail to realize what really needs doing. Jesus spoke into just such a situation 2,000 years ago when he said:

> 'Come to me, all you that are weary and are carrying heavy burdens, and I will give you rest. Take my yoke upon you, and learn from me; for I am gentle and humble in heart, and you will find rest for your souls. For my yoke is easy, and my burden is light.' (Matthew 11.28–30)

Though we usually see 'following Christ' as being a demanding way of life, the truth is that when we dare to follow his way and embrace his priorities, life actually becomes *less* anxious. Costly yes, yet restful also. This truth turned up in a surprising way in the research on what constitutes a healthy church. Those of us listening to the stories of the 25 (numerically) growing churches had, subconsciously, assumed that they were simply churches which were running faster and working harder than other churches. What was discovered was that such churches are 'focused rather than frantic'. Moreover, their focus was on the things that mattered most: more on the *important* than the *urgent*. They had discovered the secret of 'doing a few things and doing them well'.[3]

So how might churches, clergy and people who recognize that they are more 'frantic than focused' set about addressing this ailment? Simply admitting the fact is an enormous first step. Failure to do so is likely to drive the church, and all involved in it, into exhaustion and an awareness that little is being achieved despite all our efforts. So stopping is vital. Stopping, that is, long enough to take stock and plan how to bring about a 'return to the heart' of 'what it's all about'.

Several things can help to bring about that stopping.

The first is to recognize the distinction between 'doing' and 'being'. For personal as well as corporate health we need to get a balance between these two poles of human existence. The Greek philosopher Socrates said over two thousand years ago that 'the unexamined life is not worth living'. So one of the first steps that a church, and individuals involved in it, can take to 'return to the heart' of what it's all about, is to dare to stop. The purpose of that stopping is to take stock, to evaluate the situation and then identify where energies and attention need to be put. It is tough to do this, especially when a church is not used to it, but ways need to be found to bring it about. Becoming a *reflective* church is good news for members as well as faith communities.

The second step is to look for ways of building stopping into personal and corporate life. Pausing for reflection after the readings from scripture in worship (at least one minute – timed!) and making time in the intercessions help to shift the culture. Similarly, getting the PCC to stop to reflect and pray, both in the meeting and in more agenda-free 'days away' can also aid this process. Reading is another way of helping ourselves, others and whole groups to slow down enough to discern some God-given priorities for our churches and our part in them. One particularly helpful way of 'reading' is to adopt a study book in a group, and especially a leadership group.[4]

Having, perhaps once a term, an 'agenda-free' meeting of leaders in which to reflect on 'what it's all about' can also help. Encouraging clergy to build reflection time (a study day a month, for example) is a good move. Clergy need to exercise self-discipline to achieve this. However, where lay leaders (e.g. wardens) specifically encourage such a practice, that can be a great spur to clergy doing so. One of the important points for such stopping, by all concerned, is to discern how to re-balance church life with a focus on the *being* end of the spectrum.

The third thing that can help may be the most difficult – saying 'No'! Most of us like to please others, and it is probably particularly so for clergy. Yet 'No' is a vital word. It includes saying 'Not now' or 'Not me'. But it does also involve daring to say 'No'. This is made easier once we are clear about what God is wanting us to do, for that gives us a pathway from which we can more easily spot distraction. Like Nehemiah, we need to be able to say: 'I am doing a great work and cannot come down' (Nehemiah 6.3): though we would probably want to find a different way of saying it!

In doing this, it is good to remember, as the words of Jesus quoted above remind us, that stillness, in the final issue, is good news for hectic people. Some might find it scary, but many do actually hunger for a more balanced life. A church doing that will be good news to them; which is an added reason to begin with this step. In fact, stopping is one of the ways in which the 'Up to God', 'In to one another' and 'Out to the world around' come together in one action – that of being inactive![5]

As we stop to pray, reflect and think, we will then come across other obstacles to 'returning to the heart' – namely, a whole series of ways in which our thinking about ourselves and the situations confronting our churches are often distorted and lead us off track. We need to be aware of these unhealthy 'mental models'.

Blurred vision

There is a whole different type of pressure or distraction from the tyranny of the urgent. It is that which comes from not thinking straight, or not thinking theologically. There are a number of defective 'mental models' which can block our pathway to focusing on the knowledge of God. A 'mental model' is an often subconscious assumption which we bring to any situation. Some of the more common ones I have observed at work in churches are as follows.

Silo thinking

This describes a widespread tendency in church life to put different activities into different mental compartments usually shaped by secular thinking and practices rather than by good theology. Most churches can operate within a spiritual framework at a 'quiet day' but then lose connection with that understanding when it comes to handling finances (usually looked at from a 'fund-raising' perspective), or when operating as a PCC (usually from a secular 'meetings mentality' rather than from any clear Christian perspective). Equally, when seeking to engage in service to the local community, for example by setting up a Senior Citizens Luncheon

Club or a parent and toddler group, the church uses a secular, 'social services' template. Such an approach assumes that faith has nothing distinctive to bring to the service of others.[6] Equally, when it comes to addressing some issue in the life of the church, the whole approach is likely to be simply a management problem-solving approach. The spiritual dimension is not brought into play at all. A Christian approach would start with questions about what God is calling us to be and do in any situation.

Thinking organizationally rather than organically

We live in a bureaucratic and box-ticking culture in which we instinctively, and through the influence and training of that culture, think in mechanical terms. This shapes how we approach Church, which we see as an organization – a machine that needs 'fixing'. But the Church, although it has organization, is not an organization. It is a living organism. The Body, the Bride of Christ, the True Vine, a Royal Priesthood are some of the images used in scripture to describe the Church. They are all images of a *living organism*. We cannot approach a living organism as if it were a machine. Nor can we do justice to the Church if we do not see it is a living network of relationships.

This can often be seen in Mission Action Plans (MAPs). For example, in relation to worship, almost invariably the focus is on changing *organizational* matters such as liturgical form, time or some other practical matter. These may well need dealing with, but the really important elements in worship are not the *structures* so much as the *attitudes* with which worship is led and in which worshippers participate. Those deeper, spiritual, communal and organic matters get missed because the church is looking through the lens of organizational change alone. This is not because MAPs are wrong or unhelpful; the problem is in our approach to them. Rightly handled they can, and indeed have, brought fresh vision, focus and creativity to many churches.[7]

> It is not primarily strategies or structures we need, so much as a transformation of consciousness. We need a new way of seeing and imagining.[8]

Indeed, having been a consultant to over fifty churches about developing MAPs, my experience is that organizational thinking seriously shapes how most churches view reality. The planned changes are around 90 per cent *organizational* change, rather than changing *attitudes* or the quality of what is being done. It may be that the 'action' at the heart of MAPs has contributed to this tendency. However, what is vital to grasp is the fact that

Changing formal structures is not the same as changing norms, habits, skills and beliefs.[9]

A striking image from the book of Revelation is that of the angel of the Church. This is an image that points to the church as having a distinctive personality which we do well to discern and learn to work with.[10] It suggests that we need to get to know the church just as we would another person; to read its strengths and weaknesses, to know what it is sensitive about, and – not least – what are its aspirations and longings.

It helps us to see the church organically if we describe it in personal terms. Imagine your church community as a person and think of describing it to someone else. An exercise I have done with a number of churches is to ask people to describe the three most important characteristics of their church, preferably including at least one positive one and one negative one.

One such church came up with the following three characteristics: *conservative*, *rooted*, and *weary*. In subsequent conversation we were quickly able to affirm the health of being *rooted*, for it expresses the incarnate nature of the Christian faith. In exploring the *conservative* nature of the church it was possible to affirm its commitment to the faith heritage, but the group soon saw the radical nature of Jesus' ministry and the need to be open to God's call to move out of their comfort zone. This applied particularly to the changes needed to make this rural (largely retired) congregation able to adapt to and create space for the new families moving into a major owner-occupied estate recently built in the parish. Addressing the matter of *weary* took us into engaging with the tyranny of the urgent explored above. We looked at ways of finding refreshment, of slowing down and drawing upon the grace of God in both personal prayer and regular corporate worship.

> **The fourth mark of a healthy church:**
>
> it ***faces the cost of change and growth***

Treating this church simply as an organization would have missed these important characteristics with which they were meeting life. It would also have seriously limited the effectiveness of any attempts to bring about real change.

Confusing 'means' and 'goals'

'Goals' and 'means' are very easily confused in the life of the church. Take, for example, one of the questions that church leaders most frequently ask, namely: 'How can we get more people to join home groups?' Here a 'means' (home groups) has become the 'goal'. So I ask why you would want people to join home groups. This often confuses people because they have not asked this prior question. Usually we get round to something along the lines of it being good for people to belong in a small group. Again, the question needs to be asked, 'What is the "good" that people might discover?' 'Richer relationships' is the answer that comes back. And why would we want people to have 'richer relationships' ... and so on, until we get back to some connection with Jesus Christ having called us to be a loving community. So the *goal* is to be *a loving community* and the *means* used is *home groups*. We can then explore how well *this means* is achieving *this goal* and what other means might supplement what they are achieving.[11] As in the marks of a healthy church, the goal is to *operate as a community* (rather than organization). Once we are clear about that we can be creative, experimental and provisional in exploring a range of means. If a church can take this approach it will find itself able to break out of the 'We've always done it this way' mentality. The danger is that, in this example, if we make Home Groups the goal, then we either have to pressurize people into doing what they do not want to do, or simply give up the goal. If the goal, however, is being a loving community, then home groups can play their part *as one of the means* of achieving that goal. With that approach, we have not abandoned our goal, but – potentially – greatly expanded the means we could adopt to achieve it.

What is true of home groups is true of all aspects of church life, including – in a particular way – Fresh Expressions. We need first to identify the ultimate and unchanging goal and hold fast to that. 'Holding fast' means, in particular, being clear in articulating the goal. That then leaves us free to be creative about the means. If our current means do not seem to be getting us towards the goal, *we do not change the goal, we change the means*. We do not have to abandon the *goal*; rather, we simply have to look for other means to achieve that goal.

> A church was aware that no one from a large housing estate, which comprised over half the parish, was a member of the church. In order to address that issue, they set up a Church Plant on the estate. After several years they closed it because it had not drawn anyone into the worshipping community. Wisely they let it rest. Then a building became available on the estate and they started

> various activities for young people, parents and toddlers, and the elderly. Out of that grew a group who met weekly to pray and support one another. Without their realizing what they were doing they had 'planted' a church on that estate – in this case by a means they did not recognize until its goal, in some measure, had already been achieved.[12]

Often dioceses do not help at this point as they are usually constrained into thinking organizationally. For example, a number of dioceses think it is good to have a 'Ministry Team' of shared leadership between clergy and lay leaders in each church. That is fine. However, systems are then imposed to which every church is required to conform. Imposing a straightjacket becomes the goal. How much better it would be if the principle of shared leadership was the goal but local creativity was allowed to come up with an appropriate means for its expression. Originality would no doubt produce approaches that would not have occurred to the diocese but which would be a good fit for a number of churches. David's sling and stone suited him as a means much better than Saul's armour, in the achieving of his goal.

So the key is to be clear about the goal and hold fast to it, but be flexible, honest and creative about the means to achieving that goal. The goal will link back to one of the three dimensions of a healthy church life established in the previous chapter and so will help to reinforce those priorities and, indeed, will embody them.

Losing sight of God's agenda, gift and timing

One of the distinguishing marks of a healthy church is that it 'seeks to find out what God wants'.[13] When this happens, then the setting of a church's goals and priorities are in gear with its faith. At every point we must be aware of the dangers of being sucked into secular thinking. What needs to happen at all levels within the church is to break out of silo thinking into thinking theologically or from a Christian perspective.

> A new incumbent was installed with the brief to bring together a rather fractious and dysfunctional Team Ministry. His first response was to pray. This was followed by gentle argument and persuasion which seemed to bear little fruit. Then in the space of a couple of months one team member moved on and another had a change of heart prompted by a retreat they had been on. What had seemed, and proved to be, an impossible human task was suddenly changed by the grace of God at work in the situation. The new in-

cumbent had assisted this process by prayer, patience and looking for God's action.

A group of lay people were troubled about their sick vicar and spoke to the churchwardens about encouraging him to take early retirement on health grounds. He responded by saying he could not afford the pension loss that would result. The group were told of this response and met to consider what to do. They decided all they could do was to love and support the vicar over his remaining years in post. They did so, although the church continued

> The fifth mark of a healthy church:
>
> **it operates as a community**

to decline on every front. When he did retire a new incumbent was appointed. The church grew rapidly. When the group were asked why the church had grown they said it was because of the new incumbent. When the new incumbent was asked why it had grown he said it was because this small group of church members (none of whom held any office in the church) had, through their prayers and actions, created a climate of love, a loving community, like leaven in bread. He summed up the story as being about 'the church that forgot to stop loving the vicar!'

'Watch and pray' is the command of Christ. Doing so opens us and our whole situation to the grace and surprises of God, which is why his yoke is easy and his burden light. More churches should try it!

Inertia

There is a third obstacle to churches becoming healthy. It is the inertia in clergy and laity, and whole church systems, that sometimes gets the better of us. It is so much easier to settle for what is, for the familiar, for 'what we've always done here', that it seems as if there is no way out or way forward. It is both scientifically and spiritually true that more energy is needed to move a static object than one that is already moving.

For clergy and lay people the motivation is the same: we do not want to 'upset' people or to 'rock the boat'; though it has to be said that Jesus was considerably less squeamish than us moderns in his approach at this point.

Here, as always, the first step is to recognize that this is where we are. For us, individually and as a community, to own and name any problem is often the most vital step to take in overcoming it. Once we have taken that step, then finding allies is probably the next most important one. Beyond that, prayer and looking for signs of life and movement and encouraging them are ways to make a difference. It can be a lonely and costly path to take but is often the way to see a church breaking out of its inertia. The dynamic at the heart of our faith – death and resurrection – is good news at such a point. It reminds us it is when all is dark that God's grace so often shines more brightly to bring life out of what looks like death.

Conclusion

So, often the first step towards health for a church is that of owning how it is constrained by the tyranny of the urgent, by false ways of seeing things, or by sheer inertia. In terms of the marks of a healthy church it is likely to lead us into *facing the cost of change and growth*. Addressing this will help considerably towards coming out the other side with stories of grace and God's surprises.

This very process will lead into the outworking of our relationship to God in the 'Up', 'In' and 'Out' dimensions of life and Christian living. In this sense the destination and the journey are the same. Choosing to break out of the constraints does enable people and churches to become more whole people and more whole communities who reflect more of the grace of God, discovering deeper levels of fulfilment in the service of God whose service is perfect freedom.

If we are to make such a journey we will need to draw on the riches of our heritage, to which we now turn our attention.

Connecting with God 2: *Discernment*

One of the best ways to overcome the obstacles explored in this chapter is to help the church be at home in seeking the mind of God. One way of doing this is by introducing, and helping people to become familiar and at home with, a *'liturgy of discernment'*. Runcorn offers the follow practical example of such an approach that is suitable for leadership groups and church business meetings. It draws on the work of Mark Yaconelli[14] and involves the following steps. Runcorn writes:

> It starts with a simple 'gathering ritual' – a consecration of the meeting and time to God.
>
> There follows a time of relating, where each person is offered two minutes to respond to the question, 'How are you?'
>
> After this listening to each other there follows a time of silence in which the centre is now God and his presence.
>
> The meeting is now ready to share its business and comes to the task in a new spirit. The significant insistence is that the community needs time to be present to each other and to God if they are to discern the ways forward. Instead of meetings where 'opening in prayer' is a Christian reflex that makes little impact on the meeting that follows, here is a method of meeting *in prayer*. A minister friend tells how Yaconelli's simple suggestions transformed the atmosphere and effectiveness of her church council meetings.[15]

Great though this 'liturgy' is, especially for groups of half a dozen or fewer, it does need adapting for larger groups, since two minutes for all 30 members of a PCC is going to take an hour just for the 'How are you?' part of the exercise. In some situations it may be necessary to drop that element. A more creative approach is to get people into triplets to do this part of the liturgy.[16] Over the months it builds relationships and takes them beyond the business level. If this triplet approach is followed, someone 'at the front' needs to signal that the two minutes is up each time, so that the process keeps going.

However, despite this problem with the larger group, the discipline and practice of such an exercise does help a group to connect with one another and with God, and so keep connected with 'what it's all about'.

For further help see *Part 3: Resources*, 'Introduction', pp. 137–9 and, 'Study questions', pp. 143–4.

Chapter 3
Rich resources

These are tough times for the Christian Church. Churchgoing in the West continues to decline, congregations are ageing, money is tight and clergy are spread more and more thinly on the ground, some handling over fifteen churches. One deanery I visited recently had 29 churches in the 1920s served by 23 stipendiary clergy: today the number of churches is down to 23 and the number of stipendiary clergy down to one and a half. Tough times indeed!

But the Christian Church has made it through to the twenty-first century, though not everywhere and not all institutional expressions of the faith have done so.

Ann Morisy, in *Journeying Out*, begins by telling the story of a Russian delegation of clergy visiting the London diocese. She began her address by saying that she worked for an organization that was started in the year 604. The person interpreting for her asked her to repeat what she had said as they thought they must have got the figure wrong. They had not. It reminds us that the Church has survived despite incredible twists and turns, and amazing ups and downs, delightfully expressed by G. K. Chesterton who said:

> Five times in the history of Europe the church appeared to go to the dogs; each time it was the dog that died![1]

Since my own ordination in 1965 into the Anglican ministry, the Church of England has revised its liturgy twice, having not done so at all in the previous 400 years. It has ordained women and is soon to see them ordained as bishops. It has embraced church planting and 'Fresh Expressions', introduced synodical government and made a number of other significant changes.

Not that we can afford to be complacent. That would be the one thing that might cause us to suffer the same fate as Chesterton's dog. However, nor do we need to panic. The Church's life has been sustained over endless twists and turns in the nation's and Church's fortunes.

When I was ordained, the Church was using the Prayer Book Ordinal. The one phrase that has stayed with me over the

> **The seventh mark of a healthy church:**
>
> **does a few things and does them well**

Biblical roots of a rich heritage

From the very earliest days the Patriarchs were erecting altars along their journeys to mark the points where God had met with them and to be a perpetual reminder of those moments of encounter and disclosure, though arguably they got the idea from God who gave Noah the rainbow as a perpetual memorial of divine grace.

At Mount Sinai, Moses was given liturgies by which to remember great truths and great moments of revelation; hence the Passover (Passion of Christ), Feast of Tabernacles (Pentecost) and the Sabbath.

Under Solomon came buildings, namely the Temple, through which the faith could be taught, and great acts of remembrance such as Passover and the Day of Atonement remembered and celebrated.

The New Testament focuses on the heart as the place where the heritage is to be recorded. So Jesus gives us the Lord's Prayer intended as both a framework for prayer and a pattern for prayer. It

is also a wonderful summary of all his teaching, about God as Father and the coming of the kingdom, as well as an easily remembered reminder to the disciple of the shape of Christian living.

In the Age of the Spirit the memory is central to the holding on to the 'faith once delivered to the saints'. The disciples are promised that the Spirit will bring to mind what they need and give them insights from the heritage 'in the moment'. To this phase we also owe the supreme memory of the Eucharist: 'the memorial of Christ our Lord'. Despite the perceived 'in the moment' nature of the work of the Spirit, the Spirit has led God's people to stay with the original language for such key memory prompts of God's riches as Amen, Alleluia, Eucharist and Maranatha (Come, O Lord). Alongside this there is also a multitude of texts teaching the importance of rehearsing the goodness of God through a call to thanksgiving.

Classic texts: Deuteronomy 8; Matthew 6.19–21; Luke 3.21–22; Philippians 4.4–9.

years has been the call to 'draw all your studies this way'; that is, to apply our minds to the heritage that is ours and to mine from it spiritual riches and resources for those we serve. Such study is not limited to those who are ordained. All can read and study to deepen their grasp of our heritage and make those insights available in ordinary conversations, as well as in any role we play in the church. Indeed, there is a missionary dimension to such study, for our world is crying out not simply for 'exciting' people or 'exciting churches' but for 'deep people' whose riches have been mined from an age other than our own. What we need is *deeply exciting* churches.

We need to consider what has sustained churches and Christians over the centuries, that we may be sustained for our own well-being and for the witness of the Church.

> We must engage with our religious tradition, for it acts as a compass that enables us to navigate the world.[2]

Doing so can help us shift out of any 'poverty mentality' into the 'abundance mentality' so evident in the life and teachings of Christ. There are rich resources to sustain, and renew, the Church's life today, but it is vital that we are aware of them, and draw on them for the uncharted days ahead for the Church. The purpose of this chapter is to draw our attention to these riches. Doing so can encourage all involved in the life of the Church to respect, value, become familiar with and draw upon these riches, only some of which are explored in what follows.

Our spiritual heritage

In seeking to renew the spiritual vitality of members and churches we are not limited to today's experience; there are 2,000 years of prayer and spiritual disciplines to drawn on. The Monastic traditions come to us from such a different culture, yet it is that very difference that speaks to us today giving us insights from which a spiritual search limited to 'now' will seem very shallow.[3] This is particularly so when the modern search for spirituality often suffers from a rootless (and sometimes ruthless) marketing of what is 'new'. It is wonderful to go back to what is *lasting* rather than what is *latest*.[4] Similarly the writings of Julian of Norwich and St Ignatius of Loyola are rich seams of encounter with God that speak across the ages.

Drawing on the spiritual heritage from the past is likely to take us into encountering God in stillness, suffering and sacrifice, none of which are modern characteristics. To engage with these aspects of the knowledge of

God will enrich our lives and deepen our expression of the rich humanity opened up for us through the knowledge of God.

This, arguably, is the first priority of the ordained ministry – to know these resources, not just intellectually but in terms of our own spiritual disciplines. Only insofar as we do that can we then find the creativity to make them accessible to those we serve. Not that church members are limited to what the local church can offer. Reading, retreats, conferences and spiritual directors are all resources accessible from the wider Church. As with clergy, the most important element is our own prayer and spirituality disciplines. Additionally it helps, preferably with others in our local churches, to seek assistance in accessing these riches.

The point is that the Church, in the vital realm of spiritual resources, is asset-rich, not asset-poor, but we need to apply ourselves to drawing on these riches, not just for ourselves within the Church, but for the wider. society. It is these resources that nourish our knowledge of God. Recalling what Peter Rollins has said:

> We must engage with our religious tradition, for it acts as a compass that enables us to navigate the world.[5]

Church history

The Chesterton quote about the church appearing to go to the dogs reminds us that 'we have been here before'. Not necessarily this generation, but previous ones. Not, of course, identically so, but certainly the Church has struggled as much. Think of how the Church responded after the terror of the Viking invasion when its very heart, the rich monastic resource of Holy Island, was ravaged and its heritage destroyed. It neither died nor gave up, but experienced costly resurrection and, like the confessing Church in Germany under the Nazis, though physically small and weak, outlasted the military might of its oppressors.

One of the great inspirations for my ministry has been the Church of the first three centuries with its incredible sacrificial service in the name of Christ to all in need. That dedication meant that the Church, in effect, ran the social services structures of the whole Roman Empire. In more recent years it was my reading about the Great Catechumenates (teaching and 'spiritual formation' structures) of those centuries that has shaped my thinking about how we make disciples in our day. Indeed, it was that reading which led directly to my becoming one of the five authors of the Emmaus Course material. Equally, the profound effect that Wesley had on English culture is a remarkable story of the widespread social impact of early Methodism in this land.[6]

Liturgy, word and sacrament

There are enormous spiritual riches, sometimes locked away, in the liturgies of the Church. The Anglican Church has not really had a 'doctrinal statement' in the way in which some other churches that arose out of the Reformation have had. Rather, it has enshrined its faith in its liturgy. It is based on the principle *'lex orandi, lex credendi'* – '*the word spoken is the word believed*'. The great theologian, Karl Barth, commenting on that principle, described it as 'probably the most intelligent thing ever said about worship'. As a consequence of this principle, the Church has sought to pay very careful attention to both the structure of its worship and the words that are spoken or sung.

Yet, in today's informal culture, there is a tendency to belittle liturgy and miss the riches that it offers to us. This despite the blossoming of 'secular liturgies' evident in the 'shrines' that appear where people have died, in the honouring of returning fallen soldiers developed originally, and quite spontaneously, by the people of Royal Wootton Bassett, and the keeping of a minute's silence at key moments in community life. There is a new hunger abroad for rituals that give expression

> The first mark of a healthy church:
>
> **energised by faith**

to what binds us together.[7] The growth in church attendances over the Christmas period may be the result of this search for meaning and roots.[8] Christianity has wonderful resources to aid, shape and fulfil this search. How vital it is that we do not trivialize those riches.[9]

There is an important interplay of liturgy and liberty that we need to be aware of. Too fixed a handling of liturgy can focus on the liturgy more than the One worshipped in it (an example of the confusion of 'means' with 'goals'). Equally, too casual an approach to worship can turn worship into a two-dimensional meeting rather than a three-dimensional encounter with God.

In an informal culture it is not surprising that the way we handle worship is more relaxed and informal. At one level that is fine. Yet, too easily, we miss out on the wonder, the awe and the transcendence that are often the means of grace, not least for those who have no connection with the faith. It is the sense of the presence of God, more than the relevance of the language, that speaks to the heart. Finding ways to engage with the mystery of God, the wonder of his revelation, and the transcendent dimension in worship, will not only nourish the faith of those who believe, but awaken faith in those who did not know they had any to awaken: we lose it at our, and their, peril. This is not an argument for traditional expressions of worship over against 'fresh expressions'. Rather it is a challenge to *all* worship (both leaders of and participants in) to discover how 'the depths of the riches and wisdom and knowledge of God' (Romans 11.33) can be enriched by our heritage and find creative contemporary expression today.

In doing so, we do well to heed the warning of David Runcorn:

> Under pressure to be immediately accessible we assume we must jettison anything that feels dated, is not immediately understandable or feels irrelevant. Everything is measured for its *usefulness*. The danger is that in so doing we are mirroring rather than challenging the assumptions of the culture around us. We are losing a quality our age most needs – depth. Without it we will end up cashing in hard-won reserves of wisdom and faith on the altar of 'relevance', offering a restless, rootless church to a restless, rootless world.[10]

In short, the riches of the church's liturgy, and the foundational role of Word and Sacrament in it, need to be valued, explored and harnessed to enrich and sustain the life of the church. Too easily we assume that worshippers understand these things. The truth is that those very familiar with the Church's worship need help with their over-familiarity that causes them to forget what it is all about. Equally, those newer to the faith and the Church's rich heritage need help, in our casual culture, to discover the basic meaning of the word 'liturgy' – 'the work of the people' – and to enter into its riches.

People

Canon David Watson, the *de facto* leader of charismatic renewal in the Anglican Church, and wider, in the 1970s, was fond of quoting the ditty:

> To dwell above with saints we love,
> why, that will be bliss and glory;
> but to dwell below with saints we know,
> well, that's another story!

We all know the joys and struggles of living and working and relating to others, not least in the life of the Church. Indeed, a quotation I have used in other books certainly rings true in my experience.

> One form of love destroying dishonesty characteristic of life together in our marriages and churches is our niceness. In our niceness we believe that being supportive means never speaking our real thoughts and feelings in areas of disagreement … If we are to love each other, however, we need to know what the people we love really think and not just what we think they think. Where we disagree, we need to push against each other in direct ways rather than in underhanded ways that usually result in mutual bitterness.[11]

Yet in all this, clergy and laity alike need to recognize and act on the truth that the people who make up our churches are one of our greatest resources, which is why we need to nurture them and their relationships.

What food is to supermarkets and petrol is to petrol companies/ stations, people are to the Church. Ensuring that we have 'quality goods' is our primary (perhaps even sole) task in the life of the Church.

> # The sixth mark of a healthy church:
>
> ## it *makes room for all*

Sometimes they come as great gifts, as when someone joins a church or comes to faith who is 'just what is needed here'. Sometimes they grow into themselves and their role over a long period and with many ebbs and flows in the tide of grace in their lives. Yet, each one (whether believer or not) is made in the image of God. How easily we miss the wonder of this most vital resource, people, because the demands and expectations of an overcrowded church programme blind us to such insight.

The task of the Church is to grow people: that is, to help them grow into the likeness of the humanity of Christ. 'Salvation is, essentially considered, the restoration of humanity to mankind.'[12] It has become my conviction over the years that the greatest good we can do to church members and the best way we can proclaim the faith in an incarnate way is to nurture people, and a whole faith community, into the wholeness of life opened up to us through encounter with God in Christ. *In short, the best way to grow churches is to focus on growing people into the fullness of their humanity.*

When that happens, such creativity and self-giving love are released as to make any sacrifices on their behalf pale into insignificance compared to the joy of seeing the truth of St Irenaeus' words back in the second century: 'The glory of God is a person fully alive.'

There is, of course, a 'great cloud of witnesses' that supports us on our faith journey, namely the saints of old. There is so much insight, example and inspiration we can gain from the story of their lives and the story of their relationship with God. Looking for ways of learning about and reflecting on those stories is a great way to enrich the witness of the Church today. For example, about a seriously 'lesser known' saint:

> St Deicolus, seventh century, left Ireland with St Columba and founded an abbey at Lure in France where he lived as a hermit. Asked why he always smiled despite his austere lifestyle, he replied, 'Because no one can take God away from me.'[13]

In short, people are our greatest asset in the life of the Church. We need, whatever our role in the Church, to value, reverence and nurture that asset into the fullness of life made possible in Christ.[14] Then we can rejoice in the consequences.

Grace

In a two-dimensional secular culture the divine, spiritual dimension of life can easily be overlooked, even in the life of the Church. Yet grace is the fuel on which the Church runs.

Classically, grace comes to us particularly through *word* and *sacrament*. What matters here, like broadcasting, is to ensure that transmission is of the highest standard and that the receiver is working well. This is why 'leading worship' is the real task of those 'up front' in church, rather than simply 'taking the service'. The latter puts the role in a functional mindset while 'leading worship' reminds us that it is a spiritual ministry designed to assist in the nourishing of the individual and the corporate encounter with God in Christ by the Spirit.

However, grace comes to us also, so much, through *people*. This is incarnate grace; grace with skin on. The timely call, the personal awareness, the word of encouragement, the affirmation, or the right challenge are all ways in which God is pleased to make himself known to us. Equally, it may be their suffering, their courage, their vision, their industry or their self-giving that points us to the goodness and presence of God.

At a church consultation I asked people to say what image came to mind of their church. How would they complete the sentence, 'Our church is like …'? One person said: 'Our church is like a wheelbarrow, nothing moves unless you push it!' Though it often seems like that, in fact the Spirit of God is at work, sometimes in unlikely places (and, to be honest, unlikely people) so that we have to be attentive to spot the presence of God in such a setting or through such people.

Early on in my first (and only!) incumbency we needed to buy a house for a new curate. Back then in the 1970s the PCC gave authority for up to £7,000 to be spent, as that was judged to be sufficient. We were pursuing one particular property and the solicitor member of the church acting on our behalf telephoned me one morning to say that our offer had not been accepted because there was a higher bid in. However, he had been assured we could have the house for £8,000. His question was, 'Are you willing to authorize that increase?' I asked for half an hour to pray and reflect on that before giving my decision. I put the phone down and knelt to pray. My knees had only just touched the floor when the front door bell rang. With real frustration I got up to go to the door, inwardly complaining to God that there was I trying to seek his mind and he did not even protect me from the door bell. The person on the doorstep was not known to me. I invited her in.

She told me that, six months previously, her husband had died and that, although they did not live in the parish, or ever go to church, he had said shortly before he died that when he did die he would like his wife to take a cheque and give it to me for the church. 'I apologize for taking so long,' my visitor said, 'but something this morning prompted me to do it today.' It was a cheque for £1,000!

'Before you pray, I will answer ...'

It is so vital, in church life, that we never forget we are working *with* (an active) God, not working *for* (a passive) God. It is God who reveals himself in the *timings* and through *events*. Sometimes faith is about the courage to wait God's timing and God's actions. In my experience they usually cut right across how I would have dealt with the situation but are so much richer and more fruitful.

How important it is for all concerned to act in the light of the fact that it is not 'our' church, but only ever Christ's Church. He is the only one who has died for it. He alone can cause it to live and live on. I have frequently spoken to PCCs and seek, whenever possible, to remind them that their real calling is to take counsel with God, to seek his will, not theirs. That is what opens the channels of God's grace.

Weakness

This is a surprising resource, yet at the heart of our faith is the crucifixion of Christ – in utter weakness – out of which all our strength flows. This means that we need never be afraid of weakness, or even seeming failure. Harry Williams, in his book *True Wilderness*, written after he had experienced a profound breakdown, says that we should never be afraid of the desert, 'for what is the wilderness but Easter in disguise?' As John Holmes puts it:

> We hear of the Spirit who fills his people with love and joy and peace, but hear less of the Spirit who sometimes leads his people as he led Jesus into the wilderness, where they can face weakness, pain, failure rather than run away from them.[15]

Today the Church seems weak and in decline. Yet it is in the weakness (as long as we admit it and turn to God in it) that God and new beginnings are found. In writing about the Beatitudes[16] I was struck by the starting point, 'Blessed are the poor in spirit, for theirs is the kingdom of heaven'.[17] Jesus had such an affinity with the poor, and this beatitude helped me see why. The well-off have 'got it', indeed they think they have 'made it'; the poor, however, know their need of resources from beyond themselves. The poor have an openness to grace, just as did Jesus, the perfect Son of God who lived his life open to and dependent on the grace of his heavenly Father.

I was speaking at a conference alongside Grace Davie, the sociologist of religion,[18] who coined the phrase 'believing without belonging'. During her address she spoke about the things that a 'weak' church could do that a 'strong' one could not. She pointed out that a strong church almost inevitably sides with the strong, the powerful and the dominant groups in any community or culture. Weak churches are much more able to side with, to speak with and to speak for, those who are poor, marginalized and voiceless. A weak church is better placed to exercise a ministry free from the constraints of power in a way that is true to the life and ministry of Christ.

> **A church with a fairly typical age range (mostly over 50, many retired) was aware that few, if any, local people had joined the church in recent years. They decided they needed to adapt their all-Eucharist pattern of Sunday services, so introduced a monthly All-Age Worship.**
>
> **The congregation seemed to adjust quite well to this new approach, though no newcomers had visited it.**

Out of the blue, a few local teenagers turned up at choir practice. They were rather disruptive and stressed some of the choir, though most were friendly and welcoming.

A few weeks later they turned up at the evening service, eight of them in all. They left after a little while, but later on in the service rattled the church door. They wanted to come back in. They sat quietly and, when invited to come forward for a blessing, all of them did so. The service was a 1662 Prayer Book Communion Service; not exactly geared for twenty-first century youth. Or was it? Was there a sense of mystery and wonder in the very language and strange rituals that touched them?

They were back again at the next choir practice asking for more. One of the choir members asked, 'What would you like to do?' One of the teenagers said: 'Can we just light a candle and pray in front of it?' No mention of games or activities or outings, just prayer.

Courageously, and graciously, a small group of church members has come together to engage with this group. They have no 'youth work' experience or skills, or really any particular plans, but they are open to the possibility that God might be in this disturbing presence.

I heard about this just as it was happening. What will happen, no one can know at this stage. It may all blow over. But it is so typical of the Spirit to work in a way that cuts right across our well-laid plans, *calling us to trust him in our weakness*, that God might well be in this. I commend this church for seeing the possibility and daring to be in a place of weakness – for others. They could be about to discover that 'when I am weak, then am I strong'.[19]

Weakness is sometimes experienced in churches through some failure taking place, whether the collapse of the youth work, the treasurer running off with all the money, the church's inability to keep church and hall both going, or slow, seemingly unstoppable decline. These moments open us to the grace of God and can become wonderful turning points. One of the greatest statements of faith I have experienced is for someone to admit, *'It's not working.'* That is what opens us to new possibilities that are hidden from us as long as we pretend that all is going well.

Conclusion

It is important to remember that all the great riches of our Christian heritage only work in practice. As St Augustine of Hippo put it: *Solviture ambulando* – 'It is solved by walking'. It is not in the thinking of these thoughts but in giving them flesh in real life that they function as riches and resources. In the final issue they are simply things to get on and do, or be open to receiving. Stepping out in faith is the way to step into the grace of God that meets us in a thousand ways. As J. Neville Ward, a Methodist minister, in his commentary on the Rosary says: '*Every experience is a kind of annunciation.*'[21]

How we might draw on these riches of our heritage for the blessing of the Church and the furtherance of the kingdom of God are explored in the next chapter.

Connecting with God 3: *Listening*

One of the great riches of the Christian heritage are the scriptures. In and through them God speaks to us today. One of the ancient ways of reading and meditation on the scriptures is called *lectio divina* (literally 'divine reading' or 'reading with God'). It is a great way to help both individuals and groups engage with the scriptures and break out of the deadening effect (often experienced in study groups) of *discussion*, rather than spiritual *discernment*. David Foster of Downside Abbey describes it in these terms:[20]

> *Lectio divina* is a way of praying, but a prayer where we let God start a conversation, rather than where we are constantly bombarding God with our own agenda and preoccupations. One of the things we are trying to do when we devote our-selves to *lectio divina* is to give God time and space in our minds to be there for us, and for us to give ourselves to him, in adoration and self-offering. It is also a good way to grow in our faith so that we may come to 'have the mind of Christ' (Philippians 2.5) and understand better how to live like him ...

> The traditional pattern of *lectio divina* has four stages. The pattern implied a process by which the person took the words of scripture from his ears or eyes into his mind (reading, or *lectio*), repeated them to himself and chewed them over (*meditatio*), and as they began to be digested, he responded to them in prayer (*oratio*), which initiated a movement of prayer

beyond the words to God himself who had spoken with these words, a freer spontaneous moment of adoration (*contemplatio*).

To listen we have to open ourselves to someone else and let the speaker set the tone and the agenda. Listening puts us in a relationship with the speaker, and learning to listen to the scriptures, rather than just to read it, is the best way to learn that God is talking through the human authors of the Bible. That makes a big difference to how we receive the word. It means learning to tune in to a different level of meaning. Since God is with us and his word is addressed to us, it means that we can respond to what we hear, not only as a piece of literature with our understanding but as a meeting point with God in prayer. Gradually, as we begin to understand a personal meaning in what we receive as God's word, we learn to turn our attention more to the speaker than to what he says. Here prayer expands to a simpler act of adoration of God.

In using this pattern in groups it works well to have the scripture (preferably a short passage and one that people have a copy of in front of them) read three times. Before the first reading people are invited to watch out for *any word or phrase* that leaps out and catches their attention. They can then be invited to speak out that word or phrase – nothing else, and with no comments from anyone else. That is the *lectio* stage.

Before the second reading people are invited to listen to what God is saying to them through this passage – it may be in their words or the direct words of scripture. They can be invited to speak out their response, but keeping it to no more than a single sentence; again with no comments from others. That is the *meditatio* stage.

Before the third reading, people are invited to listen for how they want to respond to God in prayer after hearing what he says to us. This can be expressed in silent or extempore prayer, as most appropriate.

Finally, in silence, people are invited to speak to God about what we see, love, long for in him and his nature and being. This is the *contemplatio* stage.

For further help see *Part 3: Resources*, 'Introduction', pp. 137–9 and, 'Study questions', pp. 145–8.

Chapter 4
Living the Christian distinctives

It may be that a major cause of the struggles of the Church in the West is none of the things commonly suggested, but simply a failure of nerve. Battered by the challenges from science, the questioning of everything – not least motives – in the social sciences, and the 'culture of suspicion' that is a mark of our culture today, the Church has retreated. This shows in the comments along the lines of 'We want to show that Christians are normal', 'We want to show that Christians can have fun', etc. In part this is well motivated. It is seeking to address the strange ideas people have about Christians and the Church, stemming in significant measure from the media's portrayal of church and Christians. Nonetheless, they betray a need to fit in to society and be accepted as 'normal'. We are in danger of losing the call to be different; not for the sake of being different, but in order to be true to Christ.

When we look back at how the Church evangelized the Roman Empire in the first few centuries, how it set about making disciples and how it served the community around it, it is full of distinctive characteristics. The American sociologist Rodney Stark, in charting the spread of the faith in the early centuries, identifies a key factor as 'invincible obstinacy'![1]

In terms of the early persecutions of the Church, the Roman Empire offered a very simple way out of persecution. It was one that was offered to all the 'mystery religions' which, in today's terminology, could be described as 'private religions'. There were considerable numbers involved in such religions, though they practically never did suffer persecution. Consenting adults could do what they liked in the realm of religion: *just as long as they acknowledged Caesar as lord at the public ceremonies.* All that was needed was to offer a pinch of incense at one of the ceremonies and all would be well. But the Christians refused. 'Jesus is Lord' was their creed and they were willing to die for that belief. In the training of new disciples, the catechumens (literally 'the ones being taught') were not allowed to know the words of the Lord's Prayer for the first 18 months of their training. It was just too politically explosive because it acknowledged a kingdom other than Roman and a Lord other than Caesar. In fact the early Christians were called 'atheists' because they refused to worship the Emperor as Lord.

Biblical roots to living the Christian distinctives

There are five major sources for the identification and living out of distinctives that arise from the Hebraic-Christian scriptures.

The first is the **Ten Commandments** and the detailed legislation recorded in Exodus, Numbers and Deuteronomy which spell out a considerable range of moral, ethical, religious and dietary laws involved in following the Mosaic Covenant. The limitation on revenge expressed in the saying 'An eye for an eye' is one of the most widely known.

The second source is that of the **Hebrew prophets**, especially Isaiah, Jeremiah and Ezekiel, but including all the Minor Prophets right though to the end of the Old Testament scriptures. Here are the distinctives of following God, perhaps most memorably in Micah's call to love God, do justly and walk humbly with our God.

The third source is the **life of Christ**. The story of his life and encounters with people, together with his healing, his teachings and parables, and his passion, all point us to a new way of living.

The fourth source, the **Sermon on the Mount** is worthy of its own section. Beginning with the description of the character of the child of the kingdom in the Beatitudes, Christ goes on to address the

outworking of the good news of the kingdom, in daily life and spiritual disciplines, perhaps most strikingly expressed in His command to 'love your enemies'.

The fourth source is in the **epistles** in which the moral and spiritual disciplines of the followers of Christ are spelt out, not least Paul's call to 'overcome evil with good', John's to 'live in love' and Peter's to 'endure pain while suffering unjustly'.

But it was not just in their beliefs that they clashed with the prevailing culture. They did so also in the generosity of their care which was admired and appreciated by the whole Empire. It was Christians who buried the dead, rather than let bodies rot by the roadside. It was Christians, in response to their Lord's teaching, who visited the sick, welcomed strangers, and provided food for the hungry. When the Emperor Julian, next but one after Constantine (who had made Christianity the state religion), tried to return to the 'good old days' of the pagan empire, it was, surprisingly, public opinion that blocked his plans. With a clear sense of frustration he complained: 'These wretched Christians care not only for their own poor but for ours as well!' As one reviewer of Rodney Stark's book, *The Rise of Christianity*, put it:

> Christians prospered the old-fashioned way: by providing a better, happier and more secure way of life ... In the end, Stark concludes, Christians 'revitalized' the Roman Empire.[2]

However, it is important to note that this distinctiveness was not a deliberate choice or done for effect. The Church did not set out to be distinctive; it is just that it was so by being obedient to Christ. By following 'the Way', their values, ethical principles and worldview cut across the values of the surrounding culture.

> Christianity revitalized life in Greco-Roman cities by providing new norms and kinds of social relationships able to cope with many urgent urban problems. To cities filled with the homeless and impoverished, Christianity offered charity as well as hope. To cities filled with newcomers and strangers, Christianity offered an immediate basis for attachments. To cities filled with orphans and widows, Christianity provided a new and expanded sense of family. To cities torn by violent ethnic strife, Christianity offered a new basis for social solidarity. And to cities faced with epidemics, fires, and earthquakes, Christianity offered effective nursing services.[3]

Today, the Church in the West seems to have lost sight of this consequence of following Christ and looks to play down anything potentially distinctive. Yet it is in those very distinctive marks that what the Church has to offer the world is to be found. What follows is a brief consideration of just some of those distinctive characteristics and disciplines. They are not intended to be a comprehensive list but rather are here to serve as examples.

Listening

Listening is, of course, a fundamental part of being human, and it would be arrogant for Christians to claim any sort of monopoly on the subject. Moreover, with the modern growth of counsellors and counselling skills, there is much to be learned from those who do not acknowledge any faith in God.

However, listening is fundamental to Christianity. God is *the One who speaks*. He calls us to hear his word and act upon it. So listening should be a defining mark of the Christian and the Christian Church. Indeed, there is evidence that it is. Surveys indicate that, when people want to talk over some difficult issue, they often turn to churchgoers even when they do not go to church themselves. This may well be because Christians, in seeking to live out the call to love God and love others, develop some ability in listening to both. What is more, repentance is a way of listening to one's self. In listening to others, the fact that we have listened to ourselves and our limitations and failings is important preparation.

Yet we all know how hard it is really to listen to others; evidenced in the way that, in ordinary conversation, we usually use the time when others are speaking, not to listen to them but to prepare what we are going to say when they stop! No wonder the celebrated Christian psychologist, Paul Tournier, described human conversations as 'dialogues of the deaf'.[4]

Listening is a godly and life-giving discipline that applies to every aspect of the Church, from the handling of money to the preaching ministry, to cathedral life and to 'fresh expressions'. All of church life is enriched where true listening takes place. Indeed, it is almost certain that no 'fresh expression' can come into being without the prior exercise of costly listening – to God, others and to life and to ourselves.[5]

> We need to cultivate the practice of listening so that it is a fundamental part of our Christian discipleship. We need to be people who are always curious, receptive and open to new insights ... To *really* listen to people and to understand their needs is a profoundly Christian activity, since it takes others seriously and does not presume we know what makes them tick. It is also one of the first steps of understanding how we can enter into other people's worlds and serve them.[6]

Which is why, for our own good, for the good of the Church and its mission in the world, we need to develop this distinctive mark of being able to listen. The PCC is no bad place in which to begin. There are books and courses on listening, but what is most needed is a conscious, focused commitment to develop in our churches a culture of listening.[7]

Vocation

We live in a very active culture in which people feel uncomfortable about stopping and having 'nothing to do'. Consumer culture urges us to spend, spend, spend; and one of the best ways to get us to do so is to give us plenty to keep us active and thus needing the equipment and resources being offered. Allied to this is the fact that we are living in a driven

> **The third mark of a healthy church:**
>
> **seeks to find out what God wants**

culture. Our culture is driven by the pressure to achieve and the often relentless pressure at work, added to the pressure to balance work and life. There are deep motivations in us that drive us on too. The need to be liked, the need to achieve, the need to own everything, drive us on. For the Christian, church can often seem to be 'one more demand'; actually more than one demand, as many have multiple roles in church today. Church members can end up being the most frantic of all.

> The leadership in one church were concerned about the way in which a number of members of the church did not seem greatly motivated to do the tasks they had agreed to take on. As they listened to these church members, the common thread seemed to be that they did not feel particularly suited to the task and only took it on 'because you can't say "No" to the vicar' when he is obviously so desperate to get someone to do the job. Having courageously faced this situation and reflected theologically on it, the leadership came to the conclusion that people should be asked, when they were invited to take on a post in the church, to pray about the invitation and *only to say yes* if they could stand up in church (though they would not normally be asked to do so) and say they felt *truly called of God* to do this work. Furthermore, from then onwards people being invited to take on tasks would be specifically told it was all right to say 'No' to the vicar. Indeed, they were told that if they did not feel called of God they had a responsibility to say 'No'. This approach was then 'back-dated' to those who were 'in post' with permission to stand down if they wished to.
>
> It made for what the vicar called 'a white-water ride' when serious gaps (such as when people invited to be treasurer, or children's church leader, said 'No') yet the end result was wholly positive. People brought a sense of call, and vision, to the task. The great majority exceeded any reasonable expectations of the sacrifices they were willing to make to do the task and they became the source of inspiration for the way all church members devoted themselves to the tasks they took on. The focus on *vocation* structured into the life of the church was credited with turning around the life of this church.
>
> Later on, this church took a further step forward by adding a written job description for every task undertaken in the life of the church. When someone was taking on a new task they would be given the job description of the previous

> post holder and invited to re-write it for their new role. This
> meant that they were filling their own shoes, not someone
> else's. It was also a good way, as the leadership discovered,
> to uncover, at the outset, where any misconceptions or
> disagreements might later emerge.

This emphasis on vocation applies equally to the church as a community,
not just to individuals in it. This can be seen in the way in which churches
approach the development of Mission Action Plans (MAPs) which a
number of dioceses now ask churches to do. Often, shaped by 'silo
thinking', churches think of the Church as an organization and use MAPs,
essentially, to express what they plan to do for God. However, when part
of true listening, they can be life-giving processes. Indeed, this 'listening
out for God', that combines listening and vocation, is the very basis of the
pastoral cycle addressed in Chapter 10. It is the essential starting point for
the development of 'fresh expressions'. For Church, in all its forms, the art
lies in keeping that listening out for vocation as a permanent dynamic over
the years.[8]

The real value in Mission Action Plans comes when an integrated and
theologically reflective approach is taken in which the church is seen as
a faith community called into being by God, and now *seeking to discern
God's call* on their corporate life. The focus is not on what *we* are going
to do for God, but the much more unpredictable approach of asking what
God wants to do *with* us, *among* us and *through* us. Here God is in control
and the kingdom may well come in such an open setting.

As Thomas Kelly puts it:

> I am persuaded that religious people do not with sufficient
> seriousness count on God as an active factor in the affairs of
> the world. 'Behold, I stand at the door and knock', but too many
> well-intentioned people are so preoccupied with the clatter of
> effort to do something for God that they don't hear him asking
> that he might do something *through* them.[9]

And as Bishop Laurie Green puts it:

> Many parish churches overwhelm themselves with actions,
> meetings and projects that are not necessarily directed by
> careful theological reflection, and may in fact be a squandering
> of their energies and resources rather than a faithful
> commitment to engage incarnationally with God in the world.[10]

Churches, therefore, can practise living out of a sense of vocation by
actively seeking to find out what God wants. Once they start doing this,

individual members of the church are drawn into this approach to their own lives. *Corporate openness to vocation stimulates personal living out of a sense of call from God.*

> The Sheffield diocese took this vocational approach for the whole diocese in inviting myself and the, then, archdeacon of Doncaster to develop a way of helping churches to discover what God was calling them to do. A 16-page booklet, entitled *Discerning Church Vocation*, emerged out of this process. At its heart was a double listening: first to the local community, through meeting key leaders, and then in prayerful discernment of what God was calling the church to focus its energies upon. The whole process was then rolled out across the diocese with the great majority of churches participating in this approach. A summary of this approach is to be found in the Resources section (pages 197–8).

Being

Our frenetic culture is in danger of turning us from human *beings* into human *doings* unable to be still; indeed frightened of stillness and silence. We are urgently in need of a rebalancing of life. Just as Western culture is having to come to terms, painfully, with having spent more than we have, it can be argued that we have also run up a huge deficit of being. This often drives us to live nostalgically in the past or anxiously in the future.

> **The seventh mark of a healthy church:**
>
> it ***does a few things and does them well***

Enjoying the present moment is what we find most difficult. Yet the present moment is the only one we ever get to live in. It is in this moment that we are able to enjoy, and be enjoined to, the beauty of this world, of colour, sights, sounds and the wonders of creation and human creativity. It is in the present moment alone that we can relate to God and to other human beings. What a blessing our churches would be to all their members if they could accentuate personal and corporate *being*. Indeed, it would not just be good for church members but they might well become places of peace and tranquillity in every community. Many find in our buildings that sense of timeless being and stillness. How wonderful if they could find it in our company too!

Mark Yaconelli is a leading youth ministry consultant in America. His story is told in his book *Contemplative Youth Ministry*.[11] The title startles because 'contemplative' and 'youth' are not words normally found together. Youth ministry is assumed to require unrelentingly extrovert energy. The early years of ministry left Yaconelli on the edge of a breakdown in his ever more anxious search for numerical results. With the help of a wise counsellor he reassessed his whole approach. The discovery of contemplative spirituality completely changed his approach to prayer and ministry. It became the healing and sustaining centre of his approach to mission and ministry. He described the contemplative tradition as 'medicine to a church culture obsessed with trends, efficiency, techniques and bullet-point results'.[12]

This contemplative approach to ministry may well provide the way into so much good in and through the life of the church. It would seem to be of particular relevance and help to the establishing of 'fresh expressions'. This will not happen just by wishing it were so, or hoping it will be so. As John Ruskin put it: 'Quality is never an accident; it is always the result of intelligent effort.' So we need to think about how we might set about developing these distinctive marks.

Developing the distinctives

Each of these, and other distinctive expressions of the faith will benefit greatly from a deliberate plan to develop their expression. Moreover, doing so will not just enrich the life of the church, but will help to enrich the lives of the individual people involved. In turn this will spill over into the church's mission and engagement with the wider world. Grace is likely to be spread abroad by such focused action. The outline plan set out below will doubtless need adapting to local needs and skills. It is not intended as a rigid plan but rather as the outline for ways in which these distinctive disciplines might be developed.

Decide

Develop a plan to strengthen the distinctives. It will be best, indeed necessary, to focus on just one for a season rather than take a scatter-gun approach to all of them. Decisions will need to be made about which one to work on first and who is to develop plans. This is best done by a small group with the skills and timescale to do some reading and conversation[13] to find out as much as possible about what works and how it might be best to proceed.

Consult early

This includes both church leadership groups (such as PCC and Ministry Team) and the whole congregation. The latter may involve, for example, putting something in the weekly notice sheets informing people about what the church is looking to focus on and inviting anyone with skills, experience or ideas to make contact. This works best with a generous lead time. So, for example, a church's leadership might decide over the course of the summer months which distinctive it will seek to develop in the coming year. Then, in the autumn, the church will be informed and invited to make suggestions and contributions, during that preparation, research and planning period, to the group preparing for the focus on the chosen distinctive mark of the faith.

Look for diversity

No one 'technique' is likely to connect with everyone, so it is good to have a variety of approaches in the plan. Equally, no one way of communicating on the subject (e.g. preaching, home group study guides, etc.) will connect with everyone, so it is a matter of 'By *all* means save *some*'.

Identify outcomes

This is not easy since practices like 'listening' are difficult to measure. However, we can often measure associated activities. For example, with 'spirituality', are more people talking about the spiritual life, are more attending prayer gatherings and quiet days, etc.? They are imperfect measures but they do point to something. If there are people with market research skills that can be drawn upon, it should be possible to develop a 'before and after' questionnaire that would help here.

> A priest was concerned about the relatively low level of spiritual life in her church and wondered what to do about it. She had observed that people were often able to enter church congregations but struggled to progress further in their relationship with God. She decided to embark on a professional doctorate to explore these observations further.[14] In order to measure growth, she first sketched out her ideas of what spiritual maturity might look like. Eventually she decided to run a course in two ways. One was to do an experiential course on prayer for ten weeks.[15] The other was to preach the same material as a sermon series. She mainly used 'qualitative research' methods which look at a phenomenon in depth with a restricted number of participants rather than the easier, statistical work of measuring

quantity. For both course and sermon series she used a 'before' and 'after' questionnaire. She was heartened to discover that there were clear signs of a growth towards a more mature faith (using the criteria she had established) in a number of ways. These emerged both in questionnaire results and in the interviews with the parishioners who had attended the courses. Having moved to a new parish and completed the doctorate, she is now looking to apply these insights to her new parish. This includes developing a questionnaire that can be used 'before' and 'after'. This may be in two forms: a simpler one that can be filled up by worshippers at the end of a Sunday service and a fuller one that could be used in pastoral visits.

Whole-system infection

The goal needs to be seen in terms of changing the *culture* of the church into 'listening', 'spirituality' or whatever the focus is. So the goal must be to let this theme reach every part of church life, including the youth group, the finance and fabric teams, the PCC, the way worship is conducted and how we handle conflict. This is not about sticking something else onto the church's programme, but changing the ethos of the whole.[16]

Keep going

Doing a piece of work like this works best if there is a defined period for the focus. A year is probably the minimum length. However, there needs to be an openness to continuing for longer if that proves too short for the whole church to be 'into' this characteristic. Also, plans need to be in place to continue this focus even if at a less visible level. It is good to remember that 'most people overestimate what they can achieve in one year and underestimate what they can achieve in five years'. The real test of when the focus needs to stop is when there is clear evidence that a change in culture and perspective has taken place. That involves discerning what is happening in the community of faith, rather than whether we can tick enough 'job done' boxes.

In practice

So, what does it look like in practice to develop a distinctive mark of the faith as a characteristic of the Church? The following story, of a church seeking to become a listening church, puts flesh on the answer to that question.[17]

One busy village church had just completed a three-year Mission Action Plan. In looking to develop another one for the next three years, the leadership were aware that the church was already probably doing too much, so did not want to take on more. They also recognized that the church was not good at listening to the local community. Not least, they were aware that their language did not connect well with that community.

Wisely, they decided, in effect, to put the emphasis on *being* rather than *doing* focused around the theme of *listening*. They held an Away Day for the PCC and others at which they sought to identify what listening might involve. Four particular compass-points emerged; namely, that there was a need to develop the church's ability to listen to *God*, *ourselves*, *people at church* and *people outside church*.

Out of these plans a considerable range of possible actions was identified. They included prayer walks, quiet days, guided reading, exploring more inventive ways of praying, doing the 'Soul Spark' course[18] and the Acorn Healing Trust's 'Listening' course. Sometimes the sermon could be replaced by a 'reflection' or meditation. They also used a 'listening' questionnaire with people in the area, and contacted local community groups about involvement in a Village Exhibition event in the spring of the following year. As a consequence of the latter, the church received a number of invitations to meet with the leaders (and members) of a wide range of local activity groups. This community contact contributed to ambitious plans for a Royal Jubilee event for the whole village in the summer of 2012.

The fruit of all this, in the lives of individuals and the church, is an increasingly rich and developing relationship with the community, a greater openness to what God may be saying both from within and through others, and a willingness to wait for a sense of vocation to emerge.

Some of the lessons this church has learned on the way are as follows.

■ The importance of focusing on *qualitative* developments, not just on *quantative* goals (see 'Being' above).

■ The value of having a substantial range of different options, because it cannot be predicted which ones will really work and take off.[19]

- Accepting the fact that some things will work better than others.

- The need for monitoring and adjusting of plans as lessons are learned.

- The great value of taking people through 'learning experiences' in which they are not simply taught in words, but by experiencing new situations.

- The need to press on to achieve the goal, rather than stop because 'time is up'. 'Sheer dogged endurance' (1 Thessalonians 1.2, J. B. Phillips translation).

Daring to be distinctive

Focusing on a distinctive characteristic of following Christ enables a church to 'return to the heart' of what it's all about because it ends up strengthening the 'Up', 'In' and 'Out' aspects of our encounter with God.

Working on any of these aspects of Christian living also aids the process of 'growing people', which, it has been argued, should be a high priority in the life of the Church. Equally, the fruit of this sort of emphasis is likely to be that people have more to contribute to life well beyond the confines of organized church life. In the home, in friendships, in social and political life and in the workplace, any of these distinctives, if practised well, will – in a true theological sense – be a blessing to others.

In doing so it is important to underline that *listening, vocation* and *being* are not the limits of Christian distinctive, though they certainly are foundational. Others in this book include *spirituality* (Chapter 5), *community* (Chapter 7), *generosity* (Chapter 8), *self-giving love* (Chapter 10). There are plenty of other distinctives that churches will uncover once they think in these terms.

What is clear is that work on the distinctives is likely to bear a rich harvest and repay the investment of time, effort and thought put into it; but our usual church time-frames, of a few weeks, will have to be completely changed if we are going to stay with something for long enough to see real and lasting fruit.

What is important is that the spiritual work of discernment takes place to identify the particular distinctive(s) that the Spirit of God is calling this particular church to develop at this particular moment. That needs to be followed by a disciplined commitment to put these insights into practice and learn from both the joys and the struggles of doing so.

Connecting with God 4: *Reflection*

The *Examen* was developed particularly by St Ignatius of Loyola. It is a way of 'examining our conscience', not in a self-critical, guilt-trip manner, but rather with a good amount of thanksgiving, to reflect on our life recently. We can do it daily, or we can use it to look back over a longer period – a month, a year, *this* course, *this* job, *this* church, etc. It can be done on one's own or in a group. It is certainly a great pattern to teach a church and help it become familiar with these concepts. It naturally leads us to reflect on our lives and on the ways in which God is calling us to distinctive living. Dennis, Sheila and Matthew Linn say[20]

> For many years, we have ended each day the same way. We light a candle, become aware of God's loving presence, and take about five minutes of quiet while we each ask ourselves two questions:
>
> For what moment today am I most grateful?
> For what moment today am I least grateful?
>
> There are many other ways to ask the same question.
>
> When did I give and receive the most love today?
> When did I give and receive the least love today?
>
> When did I feel most alive today?
> When did I most feel life drained out of me?
>
> When today did I have the greatest sense of belonging to myself, others, God and the universe?
> When did I have the least sense of belonging?
>
> When was I happiest today?
> When was I saddest?
>
> What was today's high point?
> What was today's low point?
>
> Then we share these two moments with each other. Usually the entire process takes about twenty minutes. When we are very sleepy, we can easily finish in ten minutes. We call this process the *examen*.

For further help see *Part 3: Resources*, 'Introduction', pp. 137–9 and, 'Study questions', pp. 149–52.

Part 2:
Practicalities

Chapter 5
Nurturing spirituality

Introduction

If the business of the Church is to communicate and give expression to the knowledge of God, then the vital question is: 'Yes, but how?' How can we help people, and whole church communities, discover and grow in their relationship to God? This is the question that this chapter explores. What is offered is a range of actions that have the potential to move people forward. However, there are some important preliminaries to consider about how we define spirituality, about what is distinctive about a Christian spirituality, about the need for a fully engaged spirituality and about where the focus should be for developing a church's spiritual life.

A defining moment

'Spirituality' is a vague and slippery term, so some definitions will help us to be clear about what we are handling and seeking to work with. Spirituality is a buzz-word today, with many celebrities describing themselves as being a 'spiritual person'. We often hear people say, 'I am not religious but I am a spiritual person.' In these comments 'spirituality' means something about the non-material dimension of life and about how we may connect with the depths within ourselves. The Catholic priest, Gerald Brocollo, uses a basic definition of spirituality as 'how I make sense of life'.[1] Matthew Fox defines it in terms of 'how microcosm links with macrocosm'.[2]

This hunger for making sense of life and connecting with a larger reality than simply myself and the material world stems, in significant measure, from our postmodern culture. In the last century and a half, humanity has seen amazing scientific advances, resulting in the harnessing of electricity, the invention of the combustion engine, the telephone, television and internet communication – and much more. They have all had a profound effect upon how we live and see life. They are the results of remarkable scientific advances and the analysis of the dynamics, particularly at the microscopic level. We have taken creation apart to find out how it works and then harnessed what we have learned. The splitting of the atom is the ultimate symbol of this process. Nor is this restricted to the physical universe. Disciplines such as sociology and psychology have been looking at community and personal identity. All this 'taking apart' of reality means that

> People feel disjointed, out of tune with their physical envi-
> ronment, out of touch with other people, and even unable to
> come to terms with themselves.[3]

Now there is a hunger to 'put life back together again', to find what connects and animates life. *Spirituality is simply an expression of the hunger to discover meaning, purpose and an overarching vision of how to make sense of life.*

Helpful though the above definitions of spirituality are, they cannot do justice to the riches of Christian spirituality and its 2,000-year heritage. Here, there must be explicit reference to our knowledge of God at the heart of our understanding of Christian spirituality. The working definition of spirituality proposed here is that spirituality is about *'how encounter with God is experienced, nourished and expressed'*. The phrase 'encounter with God', points to the knowledge of God being at the heart of Christian spirituality. 'Experienced' refers to how that knowledge of God happens and the processes that bring people into relationship with God. 'Nourished' includes all the ways, over the centuries, in which the Church has discovered what helps to sustain people in this lived relationship with God. At its most fundamental level it is about enabling people to live life on the basis of trust in God. Nourishing faith in testing circumstances is often where it grows most vigorously. 'Expressed' covers the practices that sustain Christian spirituality (prayer, worship, etc.) *and* the way in which it shapes the whole of life (discipleship, character, service and Christian living).

So, the nurturing of Christian spirituality needs to cover these areas of experiencing God, being nourished in that relationship, and finding appropriate ways of giving expression to this relationship in the whole of life.

The shape of Christian spirituality

In terms of Christian distinctives, spirituality is, arguably, the most fundamental. Moreover, there is much that makes such spirituality distinctive from the spirituality widely marketed today. One way to draw out these distinctive characteristics is to identify some distinguishing marks of a contemporary Christian spirituality. Here are four such:

A yielded spirituality

Contemporary spirituality books are usually to be found in the 'self-help' section of bookshops. Such books help you to get life into better control and to access spiritual resources to that end. Christian spirituality is about 'self abandonment to divine providence'.[4] It is about daring to trust God and entrust our lives to his grace and to discover that his service is perfect freedom. So, in the Lord's Prayer we surrender first to the hallowing

> **The first mark of a healthy church:**
>
> **being energised by faith**

of God's name (i.e. character) and then to the pursuit of his kingdom and obedience to his will. This is a pattern not just for our praying but for our living. It is the outworking of vocation at the heart of discipleship.

An integrated spirituality

Much modern spirituality is individualistic, self-focused, fragmented and often primarily about feelings.[5] The Incarnation roots Christian spirituality in the wholeness of life and the insight that all life is embraced and touched by the presence of God. The gospel is about God's purpose in Christ being to bring all creation to its intended wholeness. That, in fact, is what the contemporary search for spirituality is about – 'putting it all back together again'.

> A group of Christians working in a cancer hospital met regularly, but they were not a normal Christian Union. They were from a great range of denominations; Catholic, Salvation Army, Pentecostal, Anglican, Methodist, URC, new churches. They were from all groups within the hospital: consultants and cleaners, porters and patients, doctors and administrators, visitors, chaplains and cooks. Nor was their focus typical of most CUs. The focus was quite clear: they met to support one another and discern together how their faith could help them in their work in the hospital. They were regularly consulted by the hospital authorities, not least because they were the most representative group in the place. Theirs was an integrated spirituality.[6]

A communal spirituality

A further distinguishing mark of Christian spirituality is that it is essentially communal rather than individual, not least because it is about the knowledge of the God who is Father, Son and Spirit. It is, therefore, hardly surprising that Christian spirituality reflects the social nature of the God to whom it seeks to relate.[7] The two great commandments, to love God and to love others, are indivisible. It is not an option to go for love of God, *or* love of others. This is why the 'In' to others' dimension of Christianity is so vital. How we are with one another proclaims or betrays the God in whose name we meet. This is in contrast to much contemporary spirituality, which is highly individualistic.

A transforming spirituality

Much contemporary spirituality is about helping us to feel comfortable and get control of our lives. Christian spirituality is about being changed into the likeness of Christ. God comes to us sometimes as the disturber of our peace because he loves us more than we love ourselves and is not willing to settle for anything less than our wholeness. 'Your kingdom come' is a prayer for the completion of God's creative work',[8] including God's work in us, individually and as a community that bears his name. As such we are all 'wounded healers' journeying into God's wholeness together. Indeed, only those willing to be changed are likely to be able to facilitate creative change in the world around them.

We will do well to bear in mind these four 'co-ordinates' of a Christian spirituality as we look for ways of developing spiritual vitality as a distinctive characteristic of the Church. However, it is important to remember that in practice these four marks of a Christian spirituality cannot be treated as separate elements but need to flow together in the mix of life.[9]

A fully engaged spirituality

The outline proposed above seeks to show what is *distinctive* about Christian spirituality. However, in doing so we need to hold on to the paradox of the Incarnation, for a truly Christian expression of the knowledge of God will hold together what is distinctive with what is fully engaged with our humanity.

> God wants us to be contemporary, not historical Christians … It cannot be too strongly emphasized that if spiritual consider-ations overlay our lives with unnaturalness, something terrible has happened, and we must at all cost break through it.[10]

> If we were able to discover what we really want, if we could become conscious of the deepest desire within us, then we should have discovered God's will … The saint is the person who has discovered his/her deepest desire. They then 'do their own thing', which is also God's thing.[11]

> Our vocation is not alien to our creation: it is the fulfilment of what we have been created for.[12]

Moreover, this means that we need to think evangelistically about the nurture of the Church's spirituality. That is, we need to nurture spirituality in such a way that what we are giving to the people of God equips them with resources that they can pass on to others who ask for 'a reason for the hope that is in you'. Or, to put it another way, we need to help people to draw on the riches of the Christian spiritual heritage in a way that enables them to live out the answers to the questions which today's culture is asking. It will help, in this endeavour, if we bear in mind that

> Spirituality is not defined in the Christian sense (of the cultiva-
> tion of the inner life of devotion), but in terms of the search for
> meaning, purpose and ultimate values.[13]

So, all the time, in discerning and designing the nurturing of faith, we need to have in the back of our minds the question, 'Is this the best way to help people live out and pass on the faith in their setting in life?'

What follows are a number of steps, or areas, in the life of a church that are likely to help in the work of developing the spiritual life of individuals and the church community as a whole. However, it is important to see the task as one, not just as a list of options or activities; effectiveness is most likely to emerge if there is 'joined-up' *thinking* and *action*. The *goal*, remember, is to enrich the church's relationship with God. What follows are simply a number of *means* that may serve that goal. In this sense the goal is nothing less than a culture change in the life of the church.

Aspects of nurturing spirituality

Worship

How the regular worshipping life of the church is approached, not least by those planning and conducting services, can greatly aid, or hinder, a church's spiritual life. There is a subtle, yet profound, difference between 'taking a service' and 'leading worship'. Though they are terms that are used interchangeably, they make a great difference in their effect on an act of worship. 'Taking the service' is all about doing what is normally done, announcing hymn numbers, leading prayers and doing what it says in the Service Book. Essentially it is about managing an activity. As someone has put it, the difference between managing and leading is that 'managers focus on getting things done right, whilst leaders focus on getting the right things done'. 'Leading worship' expresses a vision of the task that is about helping those present to encounter the presence, goodness and reality of the God in whose name the faith community has assembled. It involves leaders keeping their focus on the God who is worshipped, rather than just on 'what we do next'.

To lead worship is to lead people into God's presence. Every part of the service, including preaching and leading intercessions, should be shaped by that goal. Those leading these aspects need to recognize that theirs is not necessarily the most important part but simply a contribution to the greater process of this community coming into God's presence and being formed more fully into God's likeness through that process.

Preaching is a priestly ministry, for its goal is to make connections between people and God. That does not mean it has to be done by an ordained priest, for the priestly ministry is far wider than that: it is part of the role of the whole Church as a royal priesthood. The priestly task is to make connections between faith and life, the Word and the world, and – in the context of worship – between word and sacrament. To preach is to provoke dialogue between people's faith and their experience of life. This is how churches need to measure and assess the preaching ministry: is it bringing people into an encounter with God?

One way of helping to renew the spiritual heart of a church would be through preaching which explores the 'Up', 'In' and 'Out' dimensions identified in Chapter 1.

Participants in acts of worship have just as vital a part to play as those leading worship. It is to give ourselves in openness and loving attention to God. It means bringing the whole of our living before the light of Christ and being open to receive what God is pleased to give; as St Augustine put it: 'God gives where he finds open hands.'

Transcendence in worship

One particular aspect of worship today concerns the transcendent. We live in an informal culture, and worship has become more relaxed and informal as a result. That is fine, as far as it goes. However, it can turn worship from a true meeting with God into little more than a human activity and meeting. We need to find ways of holding on to the mystery, wonder and awe of true worship. Quality is one way of expressing this dimension in worship, but, above all, it is likely to be through the sense of wonder, mystery and awe which leaders of worship and worshippers bring to the activity that such a sense of the presence of God is expressed. As one church member, at a recent meeting, said to me:

> Our worship is led in too cosy and too chatty a way. I long for something more spacious, better disciplined and ordered, with a sense of the numinous, rather than the pally.

For leaders of worship, from my experience, it is only through having taken the time beforehand, to worship through the service before (reading the reading, praying the prayers, singing the hymns – not necessarily out loud) that such a focus on God can be given. Honing words of introduction and framing them in a way that aids the congregation's attention on God are also valuable. So, for example, before the Collect, rather than say 'We pray the Collect for the ninth Sunday after Trinity', it is much better to say, 'That we may reflect more of God's nature in our daily living' – or whatever is the theme of the Collect – 'we pray ...' This is about giving careful thought in preparation so that our words lead others into the knowledge of God. All this takes time, but it is time spent in the service of God and of others, which is what ministry is about.

In the final issue, the purpose of worship is to orientate our lives, individually and corporately, around the nature of God, his revelation in Christ, and the part we are being called to play in the coming of the kingdom of God in our world. If we are to nourish the spiritual life of a church, then we need to discern what can be done to strengthen the effectiveness of worship as an aid to individual and corporate encounter with God.

All that has been said here has particular relevance and challenge to 'fresh expressions'. The good news for such developments is that informality and transcendence do not have to be mutually exclusive. It is possible to find ways that connect with local context, personal preferences and personality types in which the two come together in a fresh expression.

All leaders of worship and participants in worship need to function within the truth that:

> The Christian God destroys the idea of immanence and transcendence as opposite points in a diffuse spectrum, replacing this with the idea that immanence and transcendence are one and the same point ... Christ, as the image of the invisible God, both reveals and conceals God: rendering God known while simultaneously maintaining divine mystery.[14]

Small groups

Study material that covers aspects of the 'three dimensions' will no doubt help to inform, and form, groups to reflect more of the image of God in who they are and how they approach each other and all of life.

At least as important is work done with the leaders of these groups. If they have bought into the vision of the church as one that is exploring and expressing our knowledge of God, then they can begin to work together to discern how that might be done by this group of leaders in this context.[15]

'Soul Spark'[16] is a good course that can help groups engage in the nurturing and exploration of Christian spirituality.[17]

Prayer groups are a particular form of small groups, and their energies should certainly be harnessed to pray for the church's progress in the 'Up', 'In' and 'Out' dimensions of the church's life. This is best done by occasional conversations with the group, in which what they are seeing and discerning is carefully listened to. They can function like look-out posts or scouts informing the leaders of joys and struggles that may be coming. Some such groups come together spontaneously. They need to be celebrated and affirm rather than be feared and suppressed.

> Half a dozen people in one church, as a result of a series of conversations over an extended period, decided to get together to pray about the worship of the church. They sensed a lack of real vitality or engagement with God in what took place most Sundays. They met once a month and also came to church ten minutes early each Sunday, and sat in their normal places and simply prayed for the service – for those taking any leadership role and for all those who came to worship God together.
>
> I heard about this group from a new vicar who had discovered it and was telling me, in excited terms, about its impact on the church. He had developed a theory that for worship to have spiritual integrity there needed to be a 'critical mass' of worshippers who come with deliberate and dedicated intention to meet with God and to pray that others might do so. He said that, right from the start of his ministry in that church, he could sense that such worship was taking place.

This story reminds us that we do not have to wait for the vicar, or 'the church', to initiate such groups. It is a courtesy to inform the vicar or leaders that a group is meeting, but my experience is that very few clergy are opposed to prayer!

'Quiet days'

'Days away' give people a leisured opportunity to stop and, if guided aright, engage with God. It is a great way to build a 'spiritual heart' into the life of the church. Such days have added value if part of their programme includes introducing people to spiritual disciplines they can take home and make part of their personal prayer life. See more on this in the following section.

Alongside such group activities, some churches are able to offer 'spiritual directors', usually by linking up with people beyond the membership of the church. This is another way of underlining the truth that Church is essentially about knowing God. Also, informing people about suitable conferences, and, indeed, having a budget to subsidize church members going to such events, gives tangible expression to the church's commitment to strengthening its spiritual life. Furthermore, this is where spirituality and pastoral care (see the next chapter) need to work together. When they do, they reinforce each other.

The spiritual disciplines

Another helpful way of nurturing a church's spiritual life is through the consistent and long-term introduction of the spiritual disciplines such as those set out at the end of each of the first five chapters of this book, as well as others. *Lectio divina*, *Examen* and the Liturgy of Discernment, in particular, if embedded in the culture and activities of a church, will ensure that its whole life will be permeated by the desire for God and for connection with the grace, goodness, guidance and disturbing presence of God. Moreover, people will draw on these disciplines in their own lives.

However, this is unlikely to happen without a serious commitment, by the leadership of the church, to practise these spiritual disciplines *corporately*. It needs to be a conscious decision that has been well thought through, including the practical implications. Once such a commitment is made, it is best to introduce these disciplines first among the leaders of the church, such as clergy, Readers and associated staff team and ministry team. Spiritual disciplines cannot be passed on to others unless they are part of our personal spiritual discipline.

Equally important is introducing the spiritual disciplines over a sustained period and at an unhurried pace. Often churches, and their leaders, see something that needs to be done about the culture, attitudes and practices of a church but assume that a single term will be sufficient time in which to focus upon it. Little is likely to be achieved in so short a time; indeed, the church community will experience a whole series of things begun but not sustained and will grow weary of and increasingly resistant to largely fruitless attempts at change.

A better and more effective timescale is likely to involve local adaptation of the following sort of pace and principles.

Agree which *spiritual disciplines* are to be introduced and the pace at which that will take place. Not more than three in any year would be an appropriate pace. It is best not to fix which disciplines too soon, but rather agree on the first two or three and the timescale for introducing them. As time goes by, there may well be surprises about what is needed and what will work best. So an evolving list of disciplines is probably the best framework to adopt.

It is important that *what is taught is first practised*, and practised sufficiently among leaders that there is a common style to what is taught. This will involve leaders practising together just one of the spiritual disciplines over something like half a dozen times before beginning to introduce that discipline more widely to the church.

Crucial to shaping the culture and ethos of the church is the commitment to *practise any spiritual discipline as widely as possible* in the life of the church. Having, from time to time, a shortened sermon that leads into the practice of a spiritual discipline would be a great way to disseminate the practice widely through Sunday worship. Equally, a sustained commitment by those involved in pastoral ministry to use some of the *Examen* questions in one-to-one pastoral contacts would work well. While home groups, and all small groups, are a natural place to introduce spiritual disciplines (particularly the *Lectio divina* way of reading scripture together) it is important to practise them throughout the whole range of the life of the church. How spirituality, the spiritual disciplines and a 'rule of life' might become part of the dynamic and focus of home groups is explored further in Chapter 7.

The value of all this work is likely to be that connecting with God will become embedded into the culture of the church.

In the past, people were taught to pray and read the scriptures daily (known in evangelical circles as the 'quiet time', and by a Pentocostal friend of mine as his 'noisy time'!). Little is heard of this today. One of the limitations of that approach was that people had a strong sense of *ought* but a weak understanding of *how*. By putting the focus on the spiritual disciplines, people can be given 'a track to run on' that might well inspire them to pray. Maybe people would benefit from realizing that what drove Jesus to pray was not duty, but delight in the Father's presence. It was said of a cardinal in Vatican at the time of the Reformation that 'he counted addiction to prayer not so much the aid of his episcopate as the delight of his soul'. May that be said of our church communities.

Ordinary church life

All the elements explored so far in this chapter could be described as 'intentionally spiritual in nature', such as worship, small groups, quiet days and spiritual direction. However, if we are to break out of 'silo thinking', this exploration of the knowledge of God needs to extend into every aspect of the life of the church. The meetings of the finance team, the fabric team, the PCC and its standing committee, children's church, and (why not?) the flower arrangers, need to breathe the atmosphere of the presence of God. This is not just about starting each meeting with a prayer: it goes much deeper than that.

One scripture that was a challenge to me in parish ministry was the rebuke of the false prophet by Jeremiah who said: 'For who has stood in the council of the Lord so as to see and to hear his word? Who has given heed to his word so as to proclaim it?' (Jeremiah 23.18). In that one verse I saw that a Church Council (not just PCC but any group making decisions on behalf of the church) is meeting in the presence of God. It is not so much a Church Council as a Divine Counsel. We are here to discover and do the will of God. It is God's Church. Christ is the only one who has died for this Church and it is his will that we are to seek in all we do. For this to happen we need to find ways of practising and giving expression to our spirituality in all the leadership, relational and task groups in the life of the church.

Doing just this, asking 'What is God's will for us in this matter?' enormously broadens the horizons of any group. Moreover, it reconnects with the primary task of the Church, to explore and express our knowledge of God.

Local creativity

It is good and wise to read books and to find out about how other churches have sought to nourish the spirituality of their church. But it is important not to go so far down that track that we miss the gifts that God is giving us in this church to help our relationship with God to grow. As Mark Yaconelli puts it:

> Sadly, most churches (and ministers) are so busy looking to imitate other, larger, 'successful' churches that they don't take the time to notice how God is uniquely present within their own congregations … There is a lack of trust in their own gifts, prayer life and capacities to create a ministry … that would be effective.[18]

The task, and skill needed here, is to recognize and affirm the gifts that church members have and to find ways of developing and deploying those gifts for the benefit of all. The story in the later section 'In practice' includes evidence that this church had learned this lesson, and greatly benefited from what individuals have to contribute to nurturing the spiritual life of the church.

The relational dimension

Exploring various ways, so far in this chapter, in which the spiritual life of a church can be nurtured has put the focus on activities, meetings and task groups through which the life-blood of the Spirit of Christ is to flow. However, another whole system of the Body of Christ is the personal relationships that hold it all together. It is in the way that we treat each other that our faith is revealed. Listening is a key mark of a healthy church: listening to God, others, ourselves and the world around us.

Honesty and integrity are also important and often come to the fore when there is a conflict. *The church does not demonstrate the love of God by never having conflict but by the way it handles it.* One crucial element is in not attacking others or impugning their motives. It is all right to disagree with a person, what is not right is to attack who they are: 'The trouble with you is …' is destructive and likely to block any resolution.

A vital part of relationships is our conversations. It is in these that we are to reflect something of the 'fragrance of Christ'. This includes finding ways of getting beyond social niceties. There are some people who have a great ability in this area. A student at a theological college had this said about him by the vicar overseeing his 'parish placement': 'He is a natural in conversing with others and in establishing friendships which are really valued, having conversations which go beyond the simple courtesies to a real engagement with people.' This is a great gift that needs to be identified, valued and deployed as fully as possible.

There is one way in which conversations and relationships can be structured and used to develop the spiritual life of individuals and churches. It is through taking a fresh look at pastoral care and how that might be expressed in a church so that everyone experiences something of the pastoral support, challenge and encouragement that they need to play their part in the developing spiritual life of a church. That is the subject addressed in the next chapter.

In practice

So, how does it work out in practice to seek to develop the spiritual life of a church? The following story puts flesh on the answer to that question.

> The story began at the interview stage of the new vicar when a churchwarden asked, 'What will you do to help develop the spiritual and prayer life of the church?'
>
> On arrival, the new vicar started to consult with others about how to nurture the spiritual and prayer life of the church. The two basic premises that emerged right from the start were that people are of many different personality types and that each person is at a different stage of life and at a different point on their spiritual journey, so one size would not fit all.

> | The sixth mark of a healthy church: |
> | --- |
> | **makes room for all** |

> The focus started with a series of midweek teaching events which set out to help people to experience a range of different prayer styles, e.g. silent or aloud, individually and in groups, intercession, praying with scripture, meditation, contemplation, using visual imagery or objects – light, water, stones, etc., praying with sound, especially using music, and learning to practise the presence of God. The emphasis was on doing rather than just listening or discussing.
>
> On a personal level, the priest tried to pray with people individually whenever possible as well as emphasizing prayer in all meetings.[19]
>
> Over the years the church has done a great variety of things to strengthen encounter with God and prayer, such as
>
> ■ Quiet days.
> ■ Daily Morning Prayer in church with shared reflections on the readings and open prayer within the liturgy.
> ■ Prayer topics and readings in the Weekly News-sheet.
> ■ A group of 'long-term' intercessors who receive a monthly sheet with intentions – long-term sick, parish events upcoming, issues about parish development, etc.

- This intercessors group is also available to be contacted when there is some crisis needing prayer immediately.

- A week of guided prayer – this was ecumenical. For one person this space was the means of their discovering that they are uniquely loved by God. They have since trained as a Pastoral Assistant.

- A church member sensed God calling her to study the labyrinth. She has since devised several labyrinths during Holy Week which have been wonderful experiences of people entering into prayer as they have walked and prayed and encountered God. She has, subsequently, trained on the diocesan worship leaders' course, having felt called to lead meditative worship. By profession she is an IT trainer, so her worship often includes wonderful visual material.

- Holy Week now has a strong prayer focus, including the labyrinth and use of the Stations of the Cross, extended Compline with reading aloud from a spiritual classic, and much else.

- A meditation group – around a dozen participants monthly.

- A focus on prayer, and resources for prayer, for home groups.

- A trained prayer ministry team is available after services, as a result of which there have been some remarkable answers to prayer, especially for people who have had serious diagnoses and who have lived much longer than doctors expected.

- As a result of doing the 'Healthy Churches Exercise', the church has sensed a call to be a more reflective church.

The great thing about this church's story is that, when the priest arrived, prayer and spirituality were considered the weakness of the church. Now, the prayer and spiritual life of the church is seen as it strength. Not that this is all the church has done. They have also done a half-million-pound reordering of the church building, and much else besides, though it is no doubt as a result of that emphasis on prayer and spirituality that these other developments have been energized and carried through successfully. *It is important to note that this story has been nine years in the making.* It is a reminder of the importance of pressing on and of having a longer time-scale for real change in the life of the church than is usually thought realistic!

Connecting with God 5: *Contemplation*

What we have not addressed up to this point is what we teach about spirituality. Partly this is so because the rich heritage of the Christian spiritual tradition cannot be condensed into the compass of one section of one chapter of one book. However, each chapter so far has ended with some inherited wisdom and discipline from the history of the Church's spiritual life to aid our getting into 'what it's all about', namely the knowledge of God. The exercise for this chapter is a way of contemplation.[20]

Contemplation has been practised through the history of the Church as a means of coming into the presence of God. It is how, starting particularly in the monastic tradition, the Church has learned to enrich its relationship with God. What follows is a simple pattern for personal and group use.

Take a moment to simply become aware of your surroundings.

Allow your *eyes* to gently receive the light, colours and shapes around you without seeking to 'do' anything with what you see.

Then gently close your eyes and turn your awareness to your *ears*. Allow yourself to receive the sounds and noises around you without judgement. Just let the sounds be what they are.

Then take a moment to become aware of your *body*. Beginning with the top of your head, allow a gentle attention to move down your body to the soles of your feet. Allow yourself to notice places of tension or pain without passing judgement. Can you compassionately receive your physical self? Spend a few moments allowing your body to breathe and rest in the presence of God, just as it is.

Then, when you are ready, take a moment to open your attention towards *God*. The God within whom we 'live and move and have our being'. Quietly turn your awareness to the presence of God within all that you *see*, all that you *hear*, and all that you *feel*. Don't force anything. Just for a few minutes allow yourself to open towards the presence of the Divine Love with the reality of this moment – the way you might turn and receive the gaze of someone dear to you in the midst of a crowded room.

Once it has become familiar to you and part of who you are (but not before), you can consider using it with others, not least in any leadership groups, such as the PCC.

It is in the creative use of these ways, and others that emerge locally, that the spiritual life of the church is most likely to be be nourished and strengthened.

For further help see *Part 3: Resources*, 'Introduction', pp. 137–9, 'Study questions', pp. 153–8, and 'Leaders' resources', p. 180 and pp. 183–6.

Chapter 6
Re-working pastoral care

Pastoral care is the Cinderella of contemporary church life, recognized for its usefulness in tidying up care of the needy, soothing ruffled feathers and filling key posts in the life of the church. It is something of a 'rear of house' job.

This lack of attention and affirmation stems, to a large extent, from the changed culture in which the church now operates. Looking back at what may seem like the high point of pastoral care (late nineteenth and first half of the twentieth century) we can see how authority figures were accepted as having a role in 'correcting and training in righteousness'. Moreover, there was so little else to do that *visiting* was seen as what being a priest was all about. The coming of a non-hierarchical culture, plus the development of the 'human sciences' of sociology and psychology, both raise serious questions about motivation. The suspicion is that, under the guise of 'caring', the actual desire is to control the behaviour and beliefs of others. This has been tragically evidenced in the raft of sexual abuse of children by priests uncovered in recent years. Such factors have shaken the foundations of the traditional approach to pastoral care.

However, these developments can become creative opportunities, not just obstacles, in the life of the church. They require us to think afresh about what we have been doing in the area of pastoral care. Rightly responded to, these changed circumstances can enable a whole new expression of pastoral care to develop; hopefully it will be a more wholesome approach.

This chapter explores a new approach to pastoral care at two levels; both levels are about developing pastoral care that is for the whole church, not just those in particular need. The first level is about creating a *pastoral culture* across the whole life of the church. This looks at its basic goal and how it can be brought about. The second level considers the more focused area of *pastoral care* itself; again looking at how a church, of any size, can grow a pastoral team that can give one-to-one care of all church members. Again, what it is and how it can be brought about will be explored. Both these levels are about the care of all, by all, that covers the whole of life; not just people's involvement in church life. It is a fresh vision and will involve work and change over a number of years; yet the fruit – of a community of growing, loving outward-looking people – is worth that sort of cost.

Developing a pastoral culture

Because the church, rightly understood, is a community rather than an organization, the quality of relationships is of vital importance. If we are to re-think and re-work pastoral care we need to grasp a vision for the development of a pastoral culture in which all are cared for, not just those in 'need'. All church members need to be cared for in the sense of being helped to grow in holiness. The fit, fully employed and happily married need this as much as any struggling with life; not least as even the 'fit, fully employed and happily married' go through crisis moments. These may be critical points of opportunity, not just of need.

This care needs to be for all because *need* is not the only, or even primary, focus of healthy pastoral care. Jesus' exercise of pastoral care was primarily towards his disciples; they were not chosen because of their need. Good pastoring, today, will meet us not only at the *point of need*, but also at the *point of aspiration*, when we sense the rightness of a new move forward in life and fresh vision for what could be. Pastoral work, *with all*, should also meet people at the *point of choice* when they are at a fork in the journey of faith and in life that requires them to decide which path to choose. At such moments it can be an enormous help to have a listening ear and wise and supportive friends alongside to help us make a godly response. That will work much better if there is such a relationship in place *before* the crisis breaks. In the final issue pastoral care *for all* is the means through which the church can make good on its call to grow people.

The elements *of pastoral culture*

Where a pastoral culture is at work there is an expression of the fundamental nature of God as revealed in Christ, namely love; so, essentially, *to give pastoral care is to pay loving attention to another*. This work of paying loving attention involves so listening to another that we enable *them* to discern how God is at work in their life. It is not about telling them what to do; rather, it is about helping one another to *hear* how God is calling us to respond to the grief, puzzles, joys and challenges of life, as well as helping us to *receive* God's grace in these situations. Pastoral care, in this foundational sense, is the calling of all Christians. 'You shall love your neighbour as yourself' (Mark 12.31); 'Love one another with mutual affection' (Romans 12.10); 'Bear one another's burdens, and in this way you will fulfil the law of Christ' (Galatians 6.2); 'that we may present everyone mature in Christ' (Colossians 1.28); 'Beloved, since God loved us so much, we also ought to love one another' (1 John 4.11).

These scriptures point us to the vision not just of every member *receiving* encouragement and loving attention, but also of every member *giving* that quality of care to others. Healthy pastoral care empowers others. So our vision of a pastoral culture needs to be big enough for all to give and all to receive such care.

The style*: mutual care*

Not least because everyone in a church is at a different place, we are not likely to get to the place where *everyone* is giving and receiving such loving attention. Nonetheless, that is the right goal and we will not get far if it is not part of our vision for the wholeness of God's people. By all means let's head in that direction and get as far as it is possible.

Pastoral care is the giving of loving attention to another, in such a way as to enable each to reflect more of Christ's nature and the image of God in their attitudes and actions. For this to happen, mutuality needs to be the norm. Yes, there will be times when it is good and right that the 'elder will help the younger', the more experienced the less experienced, the established in the faith the newcomer to faith; yet, essentially pastoral care is a mutual openness to God through which the grace of God will touch either participant and draw them to a fuller experience of the love and truth of God. Who of us, 'older in the faith', has not been touched and inspired in our faith by the insights and enthusiasm of a relative newcomer to the faith?

Companionship into wholeness (as defined by likeness to Christ) is one way of describing such a relationship and process. Unless both parties come with an openness to God and each other, there is unlikely to be significant insight or growth resulting from the encounter for either party. My experience has been that I have often known that God has spoken to me in such ministry even when I am not sure if it has been of help to the other person.

> A 'middle of the road' Anglican priest was asked, twice within a few days, if he would hold a service of healing and anointing of the sick for two separate families. Though this had never been part of his practice, he thought he should respond positively and set up a Sunday afternoon service for the two families. He hurriedly read up all he could find on the subject and rang a few friends who he thought might have done something like this. Out of this he drew up a simple service. The day came and the service came and went with the families expressing appreciation. When it was over, he closed the church door and went forward to

> the Communion rail and knelt down, with relief and grati-
> tude, to give thanks. As he stood up he suddenly realized
> – he had not been able to kneel down *for over ten years*!

When serving others in the name of Christ, you can never predict who might most clearly experience the presence and grace of God!

Pastoral care is about a relationship in which we seek the wholeness of the other person; it is essentially about loving others. As such it cannot be restricted to a few 'professionals' but is the calling of all Christians. As Alastair Campbell[1] has put it:

> ... we must learn to speak of the *pastorhood of all believers*
> and to explore the idea that each person has a call to lead in
> that special way characteristic of the Good Shepherd.

What is needed, therefore, is the development of a pastoral culture within the Church. This naturally leads us to consider what steps can be taken to develop a strong sense of the Church as a pastoral culture in which all are being helped on the Way of Christ towards the wholeness, in all of life, to which we have been called. The following steps are likely to be needed to see such a pastoral culture flourish.

The means*: changing church culture*

What needs to happen is for the means to be found to 'infect the whole church with the virus of loving relationships'. It will take persistence, but just a few can 'leaven the lump', affecting for good the quality of relationships in the whole church. Here are some steps that are likely to help this process.

Preaching

The pastoral work of preaching involves handling the interplay between biblical texts and the realities of life. Such preaching requires that the preacher allows the sacred text to speak to and wrestle with *their lives* so that what emerges is a clear grasp of what God desires to give us, or to call out from us, in our handling of life. Additionally, when handling relevant texts (e.g. Jesus' way of handling relationships), highlighting the call of all disciples to seek the well-being and wholeness of others is a way of transfusing the paying of loving attention into the lifeblood of the church.[2]

Friendships and relationships

There are two particular limitations to the quality of relationships in most churches. One is *politeness* through which we avoid reality in relationships.[3] The other is the way we relate *functionally*, doing a particular piece of work in the church (being on the finance team, on the PCC, doing children's work, etc.), to the exclusion of establishing any real personal relationship. The Church Council is a great place in which to start to develop healthier and more creative relationships. Without realizing it, Church Councils often set the tone for relationships in the church. This can be done both by having the occasional social evenings for the Council as well as by the way we handle relationships in meetings.

> One church sought to bring a more spiritual dimension to its PCC meetings and to nurture a richer network of relationships in the process. The first step they took was to put prayer in the middle of the Agenda, rather than a rushed prayer to open or close the meeting. Initially the vicar led this ten-minute pause. Then others were invited to lead this time, with the emphasis being on stillness, offering their work as a PCC to God, and reflection on what had been discussed to date. In due course, during this (strictly limited) 'ten minutes before God', people were invited to form triplets to pray together (with a clear statement that no one was required to pray out loud if they did not wish to). Initially what these triplets were to pray about was 'directed' from the 'chair'. Later on, people were invited to share their concerns in the whole of their lives, not restricting themselves to PCC Agenda matters. It took nearly two years to get to that point, but it was reported that the dynamic of relationships on the PCC had been transformed in the process. It had also shifted the PCC out of the normal 'silo' thinking of a management mentality, towards being more of a 'community of discernment'.

In conversation

Much of the work of pastoral care that already takes place in most churches is done, often subconsciously, through personal conversations. Out of such conversations a new way of seeing things can emerge that affects how we see ourselves, others, the church and the purposes of God. Some have spoken of 'intentional conversations' in which we deliberately set out to *affirm* others, to seek to *understand* their views, or to genuinely (that is, with an openness for us to learn, change, grow and receive) *explore* some aspect of Christian discipleship or aspect of life. Seen from this perspective, much of the ministry of Christ recorded in the Gospels is actually the record of striking conversations Jesus had with individuals. As such, those accounts certainly show a very robust and searching form of conversation far removed from 'niceness'.[4]

Developing pastoral care

We turn now to the more focused task of developing one-to-one pastoral care for all church members. The reality of life is such that this needs to be seen more as an aspiration than a programme. What we are looking for is that the norm in the church is that regular worshippers are in a pastoral relationship with someone, unless they have made it clear they do not wish to have that level of engagement in the life of the church.

Growing *pastoral care as the method*

The distinction between *growing* and *organizing* pastoral care shapes all the practical suggestions that follow. This emphasis on growing, rather than organizing, stems from what has been argued already, namely that the church should not be treated primarily as an *organization* to manage but a *community* to nurture and grow. It takes longer, but it bears a much richer harvest if we do that. It will not work to treat the church as an organization and simply 'reorganize' pastoral care, not least because the 'pastoral care' will be infected by the secular values of pastoral care rather than gospel distinctives. Moreover, imposing pastoral care on others simply will not work. We might have a wonderful structure, but its fruit will be minimal. The church is a community, and new attitudes and disciplines need to be established. Out of those, new ways of working (yes, including structures) can take root and grow.

> A rural incumbent was troubled by the 'petty-mindedness' that seemed to be a feature in two of the four congregations in his benefice. He prayed about this over a number of months. Indeed, for well over a year he prayed and 'did nothing' – if you get the contradiction in those two statements. Then, in the course of a single week, one well-established member of each of these two churches expressed, quite independently of each other, their concern about the same attitude. He decided that the time to act had come and invited them both to talk together about this.
>
> By the end of their meeting they had agreed to meet three times a year to pray together and to look for ways

in which they could help eradicate this small-mindedness. One of them dropped out after a year because 'nothing was happening'. Six months later, at a PCC meeting, the same small-mindedness was expressed and seemed to be almost the majority perspective. The incumbent took the opportunity to challenge the attitude and was able to express a spirit of generosity (quoting the hymn 'There's a wideness in God's mercy like the wideness of the sea') and urged the whole PCC to take a different approach. Several spoke to him afterwards expressing appreciation and their long-held concern about the sort of attitude expressed in the meeting that evening.

By then, there were half a dozen people wanting to see a different attitude abroad in the church. He got them together just once (so as to avoid any feeling of a 'conspiracy' or 'in-group'). Lent was coming up and he decided to give time to find some material of relevance for a Lent Group. Eight people came (including the six from the PCC).

I heard about this a couple of years after this whole process, which itself had taken the best part of three years! The incumbent reported that this course had subsequently been done in all four churches of the benefice and that a whole new generosity of spirit seemed to be abroad across the benefice.

This story arose out of a conversation with the incumbent in which I was trying to find out what he thought had led to the steady growth in church attendance in this benefice in the previous three years. It is a great reminder that we need to 'welcome trials as friends', as J. B. Phillips' translation puts it. Like any harvest, godly and life-giving attitudes take time and a steady determination to root in (or, as in this case, to root out) a community, but when it happens, there is a harvest.[5]

The first step, then, is to commit ourselves to *grow*, rather than *organize*, pastoral care. Once that is established, we need to consider who should be involved in such work.

Identifying pastoral gifts

In every task within a healthy church we need people with not only a sense of call to this role but also with some gifts that suit them to the task. The very nature of pastoral work (normally through one-to-one relationships) is one of the most delicate aspects of a church's work. We need to do all we can to ensure that those involved really are gifted and are likely to prove good news to those with whom they work. One of the best ways to spot people with such gifts is to notice who people gravitate to in a crisis. Who do people turn to when they need help? That is one of the most reliable indicators of someone with the gifts and personality for pastoral work. Such work suits a range of temperaments, but some of the key characteristics would seem to be:

- *good listener:* not quick to jump to conclusions or down people's throats;

- *growing person*: not set in their ways or frightened of change;

- *good self-knowledge*: not least, having the ability to know when they do not know the answers or what to do;

- *well connected to the Christian heritage*: so being able to point others to help beyond our own resources and abilities.

Clergy and readers are a natural starting point, though not all are necessarily gifted pastors. Gifts matter more than office. Home-group leaders may be pastors (though, again, not necessarily). In some groups it may be that the leader would know who the best 'pastors' (befrienders/ confidants) are. In developing a team of pastors it is probably best *not* to use the term 'pastor'[6] but to find some title that is less hierarchical in feel. As set out in the next section, a member of the 'Listening Team' might work well.

Growing a 'Listening Team'

In the midst of the busyness of church life, and the 'tyranny of the urgent', it is, nonetheless, a real battle to give time to something that may take a few years to get established. Yet it is vital to do so, because the seeds of a new order of reality are at the heart of a community of faith giving expression to 'what it's all about': living out our 'knowledge of God'. Furthermore, if effective pastoral care is established across the whole church, the number of

> **The seventh mark of a healthy church:**
>
> **does a few things and does them well**

pastoral crises are likely to lessen significantly. This means that more time, especially of the clergy, can be spent lighting fires of faith, hope and love, and less time spent on fighting fires of conflict and complaint.

But it is not just the length of time such attitudes might take to develop that can deter us. There is also, particularly in smaller churches, a feeling that we do not have the people to do this work. If we take an attitude of growing (rather than organizing) such a new development, it can – like the story above – take just two or three people meeting once a term, to begin to sow the seeds. The goal is not to set up meetings, but to change attitudes. 'Where two or three are together in my name' great things can happen, if we persist and hold fast to the goal.[7]

As a 'model' of how this might work out, consider the following possible process.

- Two or three people who would seem to be suitable are invited to meet with the incumbent once every two or three months to explore the issues raised in this chapter.

- The goal would be not just to do a 'study' but to work at helping each other to live out these truths and pass them on to others in a spirit of mutuality.

- After a few meetings, each member of the group would be asked to look for ways of sharing the insights gained from these meetings and to help others to practise the skills and adopt the attitudes that have been explored.

- Each member could be encouraged to keep a journal in which they record new insights they have gained, any ways in which they have been able to practise what they had talked about, and ways they had been able to pass on these insights to others. It would also be good to record obstacles to living out and/or sharing these insights. Such joys and struggles could be shared at the next meeting of the group.

It might well take a year or more for a group like this to become sufficiently skilled in developing these key attitudes and perspectives together, before they would be ready to think about passing them on to others. Speed is not what matters, but the quality of the plant being grown through this process.

Such a team might be well placed to visit church members if there was a specific issue needing to be addressed, as was the case in the following story.

> A church adopted a policy for lay ministry to 'do one job and do it well' after it discerned that many church members felt overburdened by the multi-tasking they were doing. They were also aware (through many *conversations*) that this overwork caused a serious lack of job satisfaction. People were simply doing too much to be able to do any-

thing well. The leadership took two years to visit all those doing 'too much' in the church, helping them to hand over some of the roles to others. One of the things this church discovered was that many were reluctant to hand over any job because their identity was bound up with what they did in church. Pastoral work was needed to help such people discover what it means to know that we are loved and accepted by God for who we are, not for what we do. Here is pastoral care, 'paying loving attention to another' at work in the life of one church.

In the light of what has been said already, a team working to identify and practise the distinctive marks of Christian pastoral care is an obvious group to work with.

Deploying a 'Listening Team'

If we are living in a 'post-hierarchical' culture, then how can pastoral work be conducted? Simply informing people that 'pastors' have been appointed and will shortly be visiting them is likely to produce a very guarded response at best; indeed, the likely response will be: 'Who asked me if I wanted to be visited by a pastor?'

However, there is a way in which such a team might be deployed. If a church were to create a 'Listening Team' (or some other title that fits the situation), what those on the team would be asked to do would be more akin to market research than traditional pastoral care. The church would be informed that a small team had been set up to listen more carefully to the congregation and to develop better two-way communication in the life of the church. In most churches it would need to be explained that it might not be possible, initially, to visit everyone.

The visits would be done by the team previously developed. In today's culture the visits would need to be set up beforehand, possibly even with a letter from the incumbent explaining what was happening, and why.

Some of the issues and areas of faith and church life that could be explored in such visits might include:

- What you value most about *church life* and what aspects of church life you find least helpful or think need to be changed.

- What most helps you to meet with God in our *public worship*, and what you find least helpful.[8]

- Finding out what people find works for them in terms of *personal prayer*, what they find most difficult, and where they would value help.

- How far church relates to *daily living*, where there seems limited connection between the two, and what they might do to help to address those issues.

- How they feel about *service* in and through the life of the church. What they are involved in, and whether they feel under-used or over-burdened.

- What people see as their *vocation* in life (not just church life) and how far church life helps or fails to help their living that out.

Assuming that people were visited once a term, the above areas for exploration represent a two-year schedule. The above list could, no doubt, be suitably re-worded and re-worked to fit local circumstances.[9]

It could well work best for these visits all to take place in the same month, for example February, May and October. This would mean that when the group comes together, all the visits would have taken place recently, so memories would be fresh. For each such visit, each team member would be exploring the same agreed issue as all the other team members. At the end of each of those three months the 'Listening Team' would meet to report back what they had heard. It would be vital that confidentiality was respected, but common themes, misunderstanding, hopes and other responses could be shared at this meeting.

Enjoying the fruits of an effective 'Listening Team'

Doing this would be likely to produce several valuable results.

The first impact would be on the *church leadership*. They would have a much fuller picture of how the church members feel about a range of aspects of the life of the church. If this 'listening exercise' is a truly genuine one, *and it is vital that it is and its finding taken seriously and acted upon*, it ought to be possible at a later stage to point to what has been changed in the light of thoughts gathered.

The second is the impact on *church members*. Hopefully, those doing the visiting will have been sufficiently briefed to be able to explain why any recent changes have been made and what plans are afoot for the future.

These first two results will have built a much fuller, and speedier, two-way communication process into the life of the church.

The third impact is that a *culture of mutual openness* to one another, not least about the things of God, are likely to grow. Out of this, a church might well find that its life resonates with the description of the people of God in the last book of the Old Testament (Malachi 3.16–18).

> Then those who revered the Lord spoke with one another. The Lord took note and listened, and a book of remembrance was written before him of those who revered the Lord and thought on his name. They shall be mine, says the Lord of hosts, my special possession on the day when I act, and I will spare them as parents spare their children who serve them. Then once more you shall see the difference between the righteous and the wicked, between one who serves God and one who does not serve him.

The fourth fruit is that *pastoral relationships* ('companionship into wholeness') should begin to grow out of the mutual trust and openness created by this process. The process can then be built, long-term, into the life of the church – while giving those who do not wish to have such visits the freedom not to be involved.

The fifth fruit is likely to be *evangelistic* in the sense that people will have developed a greater ability to listen to others and draw out their hopes, fears and their longings. That will make both the faith community they come from, and the sort of people they are, such that others will come to them when they are looking for a listening ear and 'a friend in need'. Furthermore, by the time issues around vocation have been addressed, the church will be beginning to discover how to equip people to live out their faith and their calling in the whole of life.

But remember, this will only happen where things are allowed time to *grow*, and are sustained over a long enough period. Good pastoral work functions on a horticultural timescale, not an electrical one. Indeed, the development of any distinctive mark of the faith also needs this long-term application. We need to allow time for good things to grow (and poor ideas to wither). In the long run, there will be real, lasting and deep fruit from such industry and patience.

For further help see *Part 3: Resources*, 'Introduction', pp. 137–9, 'Study questions', pp. 159–62, and 'Leaders' resources', p. 180 and pp. 187–9.

Chapter 7
Re-working home groups

Home groups have been a feature of many churches since the 1970s, so they have been in existence for close on forty years. It is hardly surprising, therefore, that some of them are fraying at the edges. Not least is this so because the surrounding culture has changed very considerably since those days. Yet they remain a significant part of the life of many churches. Indeed, a good number of churches that do *not* have them feel the lack of them and would love to find ways to get them established. So home groups are as significant by their absence as their presence. In my travelling around the country in the past twenty years, 'How can we make home groups work in our church?' is one of the most persistent issues I have been asked to address throughout that time.[1]

Owning the issue

Conventional wisdom says that home groups are essential to healthy church life, although it is rare to come across a church where as many as half of all regular worshippers are involved in one. In many smaller rural churches there are often no home groups at all.

There are several causes for the struggles of home groups. One is that there has been a long slow *decline in the clarity of their purpose*. It is significant that they have come to be known by the title 'home groups'. This is a revealing name as it tells us *where* they meet but not *why* they meet! Like some people's church attendance, it is a case of 'We've been coming for so long we have forgotten why we are coming.'

Closely allied to this loss of purpose is a *sense of stagnation* that many groups experience. Groups become stuck and lapse into conventions that inhibit life.[2] In part this is because the original goal of many groups, to grow and multiply once every two or three years, has been lost sight of, or found unattainable. It is also partly the result of leaders being left in post too long and not being effectively *supported*. This lack of support and training given to leaders means that they tend to fend for themselves and seek to survive with no visible means of support. This then creates a situation of strong *resistance* to 'outside interference' in the group's life. That resistance sometimes shows itself in an unwillingness to be involved in any overall planning or consideration of needed change. Benign neglect has generated resistance to change, which is perceived as interference.

Another pressure on such groups is that life has speeded up very significantly since the 1970s, not least because now, typically, both partners of a couple are working. So home groups are now *time-rich commitments in a time-poor culture.* Giving two hours a week to *any* activity today is a very considerable investment. *Consumer culture* has further eroded the basis of home groups as it has hastened the individualism prevalent in society. Any 'community commitment' can feel a bit strange in such a culture.

Addressing the issue

We have seen previously[3] the importance, especially in a struggling situation, of being clear, and unyielding, about the *goal*, while being flexible and creative about the *means* of achieving it. This has particular application to home groups.

So the first question that needs to be addressed is 'What is the purpose of home groups'? One of the best answers, in the early years of home groups, was that they existed to support one another to live out our faith in the whole of life. As Cardinal Murphy O'Connor said at a Roman Catholic Clergy Conference

> Most Catholics in the future, apart from their Sunday Mass, will need to belong to some form of small community. It could be the family; it could be any particular parish or diocesan or-ganization; or it could be the small communities that develop or emerge from people themselves. Increasingly there will be people who come together to listen to the word of God in Scripture, to reflect on their own lives and to pray.

However, today, most home groups could more accurately be described as 'prayer and bible study groups'. Worthy though that may sound, it is detached from purpose. Prayer and study of the scriptures, as a means of supporting one another to follow Christ in the whole of life, are great. As an end in themselves they can become a way of avoiding life, reality and the call to discipleship. Indeed, disconnected from purpose, Bible study can degenerate into a competition about who knows most about the Bible and what it means, rather than what it means to know God today.

Home groups function within the church as a means of helping to build the church as a *loving community* (by supporting one another to live out the faith). Yet the truth is that one church can have home groups but not be advancing as a loving community, while another is growing into a loving community but does not have home groups. We need to keep our eye on the *goal* of being a loving community and then see how home groups might fit as one of the *means* to achieving that goal.

Once we have clarity about the goal of groups, it is then possible to adopt the goal of infecting the whole Church with these spiritual disciplines. In this way no structures are changed, just the way that every group operates changes its values and goals. The brave will start by doing this with the Church Council!

Strategies to renew the role of home groups

Now we are in a position to consider *how* the re-working of home groups might best aid the purpose of reflecting the character of God by becoming a loving community shaped by our knowledge of God (the 'Up', 'In' and 'Out' dimensions of Christian life). Here are some steps that might well advance that goal.

Recognize the bigger picture

It is very helpful to shift our thinking from being just about whether people are in home groups or not, to seeking to understand the much more complex and richer picture of the patterns of relationships within the church that are usually around. At least five different 'relational systems' are likely to be present in any church, however small or large. They include the following.

The first, and most obvious group are in *home groups*, though hopefully revitalized through the definition of purpose, a new name, and (as outlined in the next section) through the valuing and resourcing of the leaders.

Many churches, and perhaps particularly clergy, feel that the small number of home groups in their church is a sign of failure. In doing so they usually miss the fact that many members of the church are involved in other groups, usually working together in service – e.g. parent and toddler leaders, worship group, fabric and finance teams.

> One priest was bemoaning to me the fact that although there were 50 regular worshippers in the church, only a dozen or so were in two home groups and nothing she had done had made it possible to form a third, let alone more, groups. I enquired whether there were other small groups in the church. She began to mention them, one at a time, as they came to mind. By the time we had added them all up and she had done a quick calculation of how many

different members of the church were in 'small groups', it was into the forties. Over 80 per cent of church members were in small groups!

Here is the second group, namely 'task groups'. Their focus is on service more than relationships. They are gathered around specific tasks within, or beyond, the church community. These tasks may range from the Mothers' Union committee, to teaching English to asylum seekers, or from managing the church's finances to the choir. If home groups need help to discern the *task* beyond the group that gives them focus and direction, task groups need help to *relate their work to the faith we are seeking to express* through what we are doing and the *relationships* within this task work. In other words, home groups and task groups both need help in engaging with the ultimate purpose of the Church, namely the pursuit of the knowledge of God (in the 'Up', 'In' and 'Out' dimensions).

The third group consists of all those who are part of *informal networks*, such as young mothers, businessmen, farmers, etc., even when no formal church-organized groups as such are in existence. If we treat the Church as an organization we will not see these networks. Once we view the Church as a community, we will. It is not easy, but very enlightening, to try to plot these informal networks. Sometimes they arise from people's spiritual roots (Cursillo, Spring Harvest, Keswick, Walsingham, Network, etc.) or other interests (e.g. environmental issues, keep-fit enthusiasts, etc.). Without over-organizing the informal networks, it is nonetheless possible to help those who are the key players in such groups, and to find appropriate ways of developing the expression of the three dimensions of our knowing God. If we can identify key people in such networks, they may well have a part to play in the pastoral structures outlined in the previous chapter, and/or could appropriately be involved in the leaders' gatherings suggested in the next section.

The fourth grouping consists of those connected through the *pastoral networks*. These people are not part of any recognizable group, but they have a real relationship within a recognized 'pastoral person' within the church as suggested in the previous chapter. It may well be that the 'pastoral person' is the only one to whom they relate, but that is nonetheless a real relationship. Through this pastoral engagement they will, if the pastoral network is working well, be engaged in exploring and expressing the 'Up', 'In' and 'Out' dimensions of our knowledge of God. It is important to see one-to-one pastoral relationships as part of this mix of church community life and so 'count them in' to our plotting of the relational profile of the church. Churches are usually surprised at just how many and how diverse are the 'small groups and networks' in any church, even a small one, when all four groups are plotted. But this is not the end of the story.

The fifth group is distinct from all the above and can best be described as *fellow travellers*. Viewing the church as a community, rather than more narrowly as an organization, yields a richer picture. Now we need to grasp the dynamic nature of that community. People are coming and going all the time. This is literally and physically so in our more mobile culture as people move house. It is also true for us as people. We are growing, changing and developing all the time. Some are reaching out into different aspects of their being while others are

> # The sixth mark of a healthy church:
>
> ## makes room for all

retreating into themselves or their comfort zone. Psychologically and spiritually movement is taking place too. Myers' definitions of the *public, social, personal* and *intimate* dimensions of social engagement help us understand such people.[4] Once we can recognize these four dimensions of relating it is then important to discern how, as a church, we can help people to be part of a loving community in each of these levels, rather than trying to squeeze everyone into just one level.

These *fellow travellers* are likely to include people who are genuinely too busy for any of the previously listed groups. For others, faith – at present, not necessarily for ever – is not sufficiently important for them to want to be part of the life of any group or network. There will be those new to the faith, still finding their feet in this strange community, the Church. There may also be those who are on their way out, losing their faith. There may also be those journeying beyond the normal confines of church. Fowler's 'stages of faith' describe people on this sort of journey. Ideally we should be looking out for such people, even if they may resist being made 'clubbable'.[5]

Too easily we lump all such people as 'part of the fringe'. The fact is that, though some of them may be stuck spiritually, socially or simply as people, most are moving, and in all sorts of different directions. A healthy church will value all such people and look for ways of 'counting them in' simply by befriending them and looking for, or creating, opportunities to explore with them the journey they are making. Ideally someone (or more than one) needs to have a watching and befriending brief for the fellow-travellers. They matter to God, are not fixed for ever in the position they are presently in, and are part of our loving care as a Christian community.

Affirm the community basis of church life

God is community. The Trinity, as loving community, is at the heart of creation and the gospel. The two great commandments cannot be divided. Loving God and loving others are not alternative directions in life: we cannot love God without loving others. Church as community is a vital way in which the gospel is proclaimed, especially in an individualistic age. *Community* is one of the distinctives from our faith heritage that we need to hold on to and rediscover in our day. It is a precious gift we can give to an often lonely world. Not least is that needed by those who feel lonely even in a life seemingly crowded with people. As we have already seen, churches need to function as a *community* rather than as an *organization*. In a community all are valued, whoever they are. In an organization people are valued in terms of their net contribution to the organization. So *quality of relationships* is a first-order matter for the church. Indeed, growth in numbers usually follows growth in quality and reality in relationships.

One of the most effective ways of communicating the faith is by being a loving community. That is what will draw 'all people to the fire of God's love'.

Although community seems counter-cultural in an individualistic culture, it has a prophetic and life-giving role in such a setting. People are hard-wired for community and long to belong: we are social beings. But what they, instinctively, want to be part of is a network of loving relationships. They are likely to be much less interested in joining an organization; which is why the church *operating as a community* is so vital. How far a church has the feel of community and how far it has the feel of an organization is likely to determine its effectiveness. It is vital that this community dimension of the faith is taught regularly from the pulpit, in asides and in major teaching series, as well as practised in all parts of the church.[6] For example, the PCC needs to function as a community (as well as a management committee), so thought needs to be given as to how to express that.

Recover the goal of home groups

One of the best ways to revitalize home groups is to recover the goal in terms of them being loving communities in which we help each other grow as disciples of Christ. This is where the model set out in Chapter 1, of the three dimensions of our knowledge of God ('Up', 'In', and 'Out'), can be a helpful template for groups and also a useful checklist in terms of assessing how much attention we are giving to each of these dimensions; though those three dimensions need to be given substance in such a way that we can have some clear measure of how we are doing.

One church decided to devolve to each group the definition of its task or mission project. They worked on the basis that 'no group can be healthy unless it has a goal beyond itself to fulfil'. For some groups it was about helping each other to live out our faith. For those groups the leaders of the church worked with them to identify achievable outcomes that might reasonably be looked for with this goal. Other groups were much more 'specific project' orientated, such as a group built around the parent and toddler group and one that was a men's group and took on engagement with young people as its task.

At the same time the leadership of the church, courageously and wisely, said to the group, 'You no longer have to meet on the usual night for home groups, indeed you no longer have to meet at all.' Rather, they were told, 'If this is your task, now work out how you can best fulfil it.' The group's programme arose in response to that question.

The whole process certainly revitalized the groups in that church.

It can help as part of this work if groups are given a new name (a new 'branding') that relates to their purpose, such as Discipleship Groups, Mission Groups, Support Groups, etc. Particularly where such a development is linked to the building of group leaders into a key pastoral team in the life of the church, this can have a transformative impact on groups and the whole life of the church.

Re-connect with spirituality

Another way of revitalizing home groups is to shift the focus to nurturing faith/spirituality. This can be seen as part of a bigger search in the Church today which has resulted in the development of 'missional communities'. These are groups of people who are seeking to gain insights for today's Church from the origins of the monastic movement that has sustained faith over many centuries. One such way involves developing a shared 'rule of life', or pattern of shared commitments.

Lichfield diocese, for example, drew insight and inspiration from its founding father when it developed the Community of Saint Chad. This is a missional community which offers a path to spiritual growth based upon five aspirational statements called 'Rhythms of Grace' and recommends a method of spiritual mentoring through small growth

> groups. **These are now being developed in many parishes across the diocese. Other dioceses are already looking to adapt this material to their context.**

This approach is a way of integrating the nurturing spirituality, growing people, and expressing the distinctive lifestyle of the Christian faith.

Working to nurture faith through shared commitments, including the commitment to support one another to live out the faith, is one of the more obvious ways of 'returning to the heart' of what Christianity is all about, for which this book argues. Shifting the focus of home groups to nurturing faith/spirituality and its outworking in life will not only bring new life to groups that have stagnated, but puts being energized by faith at the heart of such groups.

Turn the whole church outwards

One of the diseases that afflicts home groups is stagnation. Much good may flow in, but if nothing is getting out, just like a pool of water, the life of the group will stagnate. So helping the group to discover a goal beyond itself is important. If this is linked to the development of the pastoral care of the whole church through one-to-one relationships then the impact will be considerable. Helping each member of the church to discover God's calling on the whole of their lives[7] can be a liberating experience for people and turn out the whole church to live the Lord's Prayer: 'your kingdom come, your will be done'.[8]

Resourcing the leaders

A key group of people who are often under-resourced in the life of a church, is that of home group leaders. There is much to be gained by gathering this group together between three and six times a year. It is best to define this group in wider terms than just home group leaders. It works best to include leaders of home groups, task groups, pastoral work leaders, informal network leaders and – if such exist – fellow-traveller befrienders. This is a crucial 'middle management' group within the church that can act as a two-way conduit of communication to and from church members, like veins and arteries in the Body of Christ. It is a strategic group in which to invest thought and effort.

A number of churches have adopted the following threefold pattern for such meetings:

Vision

This involves two-way communication. Sharing with the group leaders about the overall direction and priorities of the church is a vital part of getting the vision into the life-blood of the church. Equally valuable is hearing their response. It is good to know when people are with us and share the vision. It is also important to know when that is not true. Where that is the case, it may not mean that the vision is wrong, but it helps to know what are the resistance points in the congregation. Moreover, insights from the church will, or should, re-shape and enrich the church's vision and focus.

Huddle

No leader of a small group will get all the support they need from *within* the group. They are there to serve rather than be served, even though they will receive much from their groups. In the leadership group they should find a safe place in which to share their struggles and problems and find support, help and encouragement.

Skills

Group leaders benefit greatly from learning how to do the job better. Spending time in each session exploring issues such as leading a discussion, handling conflict, developing corporate prayer and creative engagement with the scriptures not only gives leaders confidence but also the skills to do the job.[9]

Gathering together a group like this is a key way of shaping the ethos and culture of the whole church. For this to happen it is important that the meetings are of such high quality that no one wants to miss them. This takes time and serious and creative preparation. Such a meeting can become, in the very best sense, the heart of the church.

> One church had a flourishing home groups structure, complete with a regular meeting for the leaders of those groups. Then the incumbent left and the new one dropped the meeting as he said he 'couldn't see the point of the meeting'. The whole structure of home groups began to disintegrate from that point on, and very little was left after only a few years.

Develop alternative models

All that has been said so far is essentially about making the most of what we have by way of home groups. However, it is important not to stop there. It helps if a church looks for and develops a continuum of groups and informal networks. Together, this variety will strengthen the community dynamic of the church. It will also give a much richer picture of the total community of the church. However, we can go further than that, such as:

> Some churches have been experimenting with *prayer triplets*, both alongside existing home groups and as part of their way of operating. Typically, the triplet is entirely free to work out how it wants to operate. They meet for about ninety minutes once a month. The focus is on living the faith and the joys and struggles in doing so. Each person takes half an hour, including at least five minutes' prayer at the end of each half-hour session. These groups are usually single sex and self-selecting. Some operate as a more focused and time-efficient way of doing home groups. Others operate within existing home groups. With these they either meet as a triplet within a group meeting, or once a month there is no home group, just triplet meetings.

> One church calls these groups *'listening groups'*. Their basic pattern is the use of Yaconelli's Liturgy of Discernment.[10] Some of these groups are using the excellent material produced by the 'Community of St Chad' in the Lichfield diocese.[11]

> Other churches have turned the *men's group*, in effect, into a home group; though again, how often they meet, and when and how they meet, is up to the group. What the 'church leaders' work on is helping the group to define its goal and identify appropriate 'outcomes' to look for. However, the group(s) also have a termly dinner and other social events so the group meetings are part of a bigger pattern.

Some churches focus on *cell groups*, and others on larger groupings called *clusters*. They are worth exploring to see if there are lessons to be learned. The only warning is to underline that any structure is, in the final issue, a means and not a goal in itself.

Conclusion

Home groups, when functioning as effective support groups for living out the faith, have a continuing role in the life of the church. But a good number of people can find that sort of 'fellowship' by working on a project or form of service together, or in a prayer triplet. All small groups need a balance of *being* and *doing*. Small groups often need to build *being* into their agenda and home groups need to build *doing* into theirs. The one-to-one pastoral care of all church members is another aspect of this nurturing of faith and discipleship. All these elements, combined together, enhanced by getting pastoral leaders and leaders of home and small groups together regularly, can aid the overriding goal of becoming a loving community in which people are discovering the resources and support that lead them on to greater wholeness as people. As long as a church keeps that goal firmly before it, it is much more likely to find creative and effective ways to function in small groups.

For further help see *Part 3: Resources*, 'Introduction', pp. 137–9, 'Study questions', pp. 163–7, and 'Leaders' resources', p. 180–1.

Chapter 8
Re-working giving

This book began by asking what Church is all about, identified the answer as being about 'the knowledge of God', and has gone on to explore how this works out in practice. But a chapter on church finances? Is that not going from the sublime, if not to the ridiculous then at least to the seriously mundane? Definitely not! Christianity is an embodied and incarnate faith. Orthodox Christianity does not have a 'sacred' and 'secular' divide, because it sees all of life as sacred and part of God's creation. All of life, including the handling of money, is to be lived before God. Indeed, the sacred or holy is expressed in the physical and material realms just as much as in the spiritual and relational dimensions of life, as the Incarnation makes evident. What is more, finances play a very big part in any church, and it is important, if we want to develop healthy churches, to identify healthy ways of addressing the financial needs and challenges of the Church today.

This is particularly so since 'silo thinking' (in which the spiritual dimension is kept in a sealed unit apart from practical realities) has profoundly shaped the Church's approach to money. Essentially a secular approach to finances that can be summarized as a 'fundraising' perspective battles with a 'Christian giving' way of seeing finances. Life being what it is, these two approaches often co-exist in churches. Where that is the case it is important to discern which one is the primary approach, and which way the balance between the two is heading.

The, secular, 'fundraising' approach is built on the view that people do not want to give, but will if they can see they get something in return. It may be a raffle prize, or the experience of the fundraising event (pantomime, summer fair or Christmas market, etc.) which makes them willing to part with their money. It is based also on the premise, 'If we all give a little, none of us need feel any real cost in our giving, or rather contributing.' Another characteristic of such giving is that, by giving money we absolve ourselves from giving of ourselves. It is really a structure for the double avoidance of sacrifice (costly financial giving or self-giving). The contemporary 'sponsoring culture' simply adds moral pressure and the manipulation of relationships to the same end of getting money out of reluctant givers. It seems almost offensive to quote the biblical description of the character and action of God in the same paragraph as this brief outline of secular fundraising, but it needs to be done to see the starkness of the contrast. The greater truth is that 'God so loved the world that he gave his only son' (John 3.16). 'Love gives' is the basis of Christian giving.

The generosity distinctive

There is clearly a profound contrast between this and what has passed, historically, for Christian giving. We have to be careful here because 'Christian giving' cannot be properly understood from a narrowly financial perspective. Its roots are in the giving and generosity of God seen as much in creation's abundance as in his redeeming, self-giving love.[1] If Christian giving is rooted in the generosity of God, it is also expressed in a whole attitude to life, not just an attitude to money. The story of the Carthage Christians told in an earlier chapter illustrates how generosity was a hallmark of the early Church. Despite persecution they gave with great generosity, giving themselves and giving sacrificially in the service of others. This is the dynamic of 'over the top' giving in response to the grace of God at work in the giving of the Macedonian churches that Paul reports (2 Corinthians 8.1ff.).

> We want you to know, brothers and sisters, about the grace of God that has been granted to the churches of Macedonia; for during a severe ordeal of affliction, their abundant joy and their extreme poverty have overflowed in a wealth of generosity on their part. For, as I can testify, they voluntarily gave according to their means, and even beyond their means, begging us earnestly for the privilege of sharing in this ministry to the saints – and this, not merely as we expected; they gave themselves first to the Lord and, by the will of God, to us.

What is proposed here is that the best way to re-work the practice of financial giving in a church is to start by exploring the multi-faceted wonder of the generosity of God. That would then lead on to consideration of God's call to the church to reflect that same generosity in our approach to the whole of life. Here, it is best to look for, affirm and celebrate giving in and through the life of the church *other than* financial giving. Once signs of such generosity, by individuals and through the organized life of the church, become evident, then it would be appropriate to move on to focus specifically on financial giving and a specific outworking of this wider principle.

> Jesus lives his life as if there is a boundless, shameless love present and available within every moment.[2]

So, re-working giving is best approached through the exploration and expression of generosity. This means treating *generosity* as a Christian distinctive to be handled along the lines set out in Chapter 4 'Living the Christian distinctives'. This chapter explores ways in which a church might re-work its whole approach to giving by a sustained focus on the Christian distinctive of *generosity*.

> One church, in its various smaller groups, studied Philip Yancy's *What's So Amazing About Grace?* (Zondervan, 1997). In doing so people were invited to look for ways in which they could show God's love in surprising acts of grace. A variety of actions resulted, ranging from decorating the flat of a neighbour, giving the garden of a pensioner a makeover, to collecting baby clothes for needy mums.

Celebrating God's generosity

Christian giving is a response to the generosity of God, so the first task is to bring the generosity of God into life-changing focus. Some of the ways of doing this include the following.

In the Church's year

Because the story of scripture is essentially the story of God's loving and generous engagement with his creation and creatures, the Church's year provides a rich source of allusions to the generosity of God. Although, liturgically, the Christian year begins at Advent, in practice most churches begin their 'new year' with the start of school terms in September. So a natural starting point for exploring generosity is Harvest Festival in which we celebrate God's generosity as the creator (and provider) of all the material resources needed for life. Air, water, shelter, clothing, come to us freely in their original form. Advent highlights self-giving sacrifice as a great mark of Christian giving, through the lives of the prophets, John the Baptist and Mary, as well as in the Advent themes of hope, peace, wisdom and joy. Supremely this self-giving love is demonstrated in the coming of Christ.

And so, on through the Christian year and the Great Festivals, the wonder of God's loving generosity and its shape as a distinctive Christian characteristic (see below) come successively into focus. All that is needed are brief comments that draw attention to this theme in hymns and readings. In this way generosity is drawn out from the background and brought to the Church's attention.

> **The first mark of a healthy church:**
>
> **energised by faith**

In the Eucharist

Not least because Eucharist means 'thanksgiving' we are drawn both to the greatest demonstration of God's generosity in the passion of Christ, and also to our calling to respond, in the Eucharist and all of life, by being a people marked by a spirit of gratitude and thanksgiving, to God and to others.

In church life

It is always good to take opportunities to express appreciation for what people do selflessly, freely and usually in a hidden way, in the service of others. When someone completes some task in the church it is good to express thanks publicly. It is good also to encourage people to go out of their way to affirm those who are serving the church in any way. Vicar and wardens could make a pact to affirm all such people and report back to each other when they have done so – engaging in a conspiracy of affirmation and gratitude. Maybe more powerful would be a small group of church members doing just the same – and not forgetting to include the vicar and wardens in their list of people to address in this way!

In personal relationships

We know, in raising children, that it is better to affirm what is good than criticize what is wrong. So, in seeking to strengthen people's relationship with God (the 'Up' dimension), when we pray with them we can begin with thanksgiving for God's generosity. When we are talking about our relationship with others in the church (the 'In' dimension) we can affirm people about any positive contribution we have noticed in their attitude to others, as well as affirm others in the church. In this connection it is good to work on the same principle as the Apostle Paul in his dealing with churches. Though he had plenty of tough and challenging 'criticisms' to make of churches, he only made them to that church. When speaking of one church to another, he only ever expressed the positives. In exploring, in personal conversation, the needs of the world around us (the 'Out' dimension) it is good to draw attention to and affirm all who are making costly sacrifices for the good of others.

In stories

It is good to look out for stories, from church history, the lives of the saints, contemporary church life, and particularly from the lives of the members of *this* church that demonstrate and inspire us by their example, and to find ways of spreading those stories around. If a picture is worth a thousand words, so is a story. One such story from the early Church illustrates what Ann Morisy calls 'the cascade of grace' that flows from self-giving love. It is the story of how the generosity of one local church was instrumental in the founding of the whole monastic movement.

> Shortly after Anthony, the other great founder of Egyptian monasticism, Pachomius, established more highly organized communities in the south. Nevertheless his goals were similar to Anthony's. According to his first Greek biography,[3] his initial encounter with Christians came after he had been conscripted into the army. As a cold, hungry and miserable young soldier he was locked up with fellow conscripts in the city of Thebes. While he was there some Christians brought them food and other necessities, an act of charity that overwhelmed Pachomius. When he asked who they were, he was told that Christians are people 'who bear the name of Christ, the only Son of God, and they do all manner of good things for everyone, putting their hope on him who made the heaven and earth and us [human beings]'. Pachomius was so struck by this that he prayed to God, vowing that if he were allowed to escape, he would become a Christian. Later, after his release and seeking the will of God for himself, he heard his own call to the desert.

Living in thanksgiving

Closely allied to generosity is the discipline and practice of thanksgiving. That is what Eucharist means and it is a theme repeated, particularly in the Pauline epistles, on a considerable number of occasions. Francis Schaeffer, in *True Spirituality*, shows how this is at the heart of Christian spirituality, and concludes: 'the beginning of our rebellion against God was, and is, the lack of a thankful heart'.[4]

Nurturing a thankful attitude and culture of affirmation and appreciation is all part of the Church's call to reflect the divine generosity in its life.

Thanksgiving is not only something we express to God but to others as well. At the human level this often takes the form of expressing appreciation and in the giving of affirmation to others. It is one way we pay loving attention to others. In the Resources section there is material from one church which has been seeking to develop this 'gratitude attitude' corporately. In these days of austerity and financial strain in much of the Western world, the expression of gratitude and thanksgiving can be a significant sign of the kingdom of God and a way of bringing good news into the contexts in which we live.

Biblical roots of thanksgiving

The Pauline texts on thanksgiving

Ever since the creation of the world his eternal power and divine nature, invisible though they are, have been understood and seen through the things he has made. So they are without excuse; for though they knew God, they did not honour him as God or give thanks to him. (Romans 1.20–21)

Entirely out of place is obscene, silly and vulgar talk; but instead, let there be thanksgiving. (Ephesians 5.4)

Do not get drunk with wine, for that is debauchery; but be filled with the Spirit, as you sing psalms and hymns and spiritual songs among yourselves, singing and making melody to the Lord in your hearts, giving thanks to God the Father at all times and for everything in the name of our Lord Jesus Christ. (Ephesians 5.18–20)

Do not worry about anything, but in everything by prayer and supplication with thanksgiving let your requests be made known to God. (Philippians 4.6)

As you therefore have received Christ Jesus the Lord, continue to live your lives in him, rooted and built up in him and established in the faith, just as you were taught, abounding in thanksgiving. (Colossians 2.6–7)

And let the peace of Christ rule in your hearts, to which indeed you were called in the one body. And be thankful. And whatever you do, in word or deed, do everything in the name of the Lord Jesus, giving thanks to God the Father through him. (Colossians 3.15–17)

Devote yourselves to prayer, keeping alert in it with thanksgiving. (Colossians 4.2)

Rejoice always, pray without ceasing, give thanks in all circumstances; for this is the will of God in Christ Jesus for you. Do not quench the Spirit. (1 Thessalonians 5.16–19)

Classic generosity texts:
Matthew 5.43–48; Matthew 6.1–4; Matthew 6.19–24;
Philippians 2.5–11; 2 Corinthians 8, 9.

Motivation for Christian giving

Motivation is not something we often think about, yet doing things from true motives is an important part of what makes an act a Christian and godly action. In considering motivation, as noted above, we are not just thinking about the giving of money, but all forms of self-giving and service which spring from the same streams of holy giving.

The starting point for Christian giving, as we have seen, is *grace*. We give in response to the grace of God. Helping people to give as a response to the goodness and reality of God is vital in financial giving and practical service.

> In a church which had been through a period of remarkably sacrificial giving, the vicar was asked to speak on the subject in another diocese. He asked the treasurer to suggest two people who were giving generously to take and ask them to speak about their giving. It was a church where only the treasurer knew who gave and how much they gave.
>
> When these two people met with the vicar to prepare for the event, he began by asking them how they 'got into tithing'. Both people looked puzzled and said, 'What's that?' He explained it was the principle of giving one-tenth of our income to God. He reported afterwards that he could see their minds replaying their situation as they calculated whether they were giving that amount or not!
>
> After they had had 'tithing' explained, they both said it was not about tithing but rather that they had received so much from God since coming to faith and to this church that they wanted to give back as a response to what they had received from God and the church. That was what had motivated them.

Next comes *vision/vocation* in which we sense and discern what God is wanting from us in the particular situation we face.

> One young woman was moved by the plight of street children in Mongolia sleeping in the town sewers at night to keep warm. She discovered that a Christian agency was working there to set up traditional Mongolian Tents in which families lived. They were able to find families willing to adopt a couple of dozen street children and live with

them in such a Tent provided by the agency. She asked the vicar if the Sunday School could help raise £300 to pay for one of these Tents. He agreed. Within a few years they had gathered enough funds to pay for over a dozen such Tents. Her vocation had fired the vision and sacrifice of the whole church congregation.

The third element in the motivation for Christian service and giving is that of *belonging*. If we feel part of a 'show' we will contribute. This sense of belonging is not only about being cared for, but having the opportunity to contribute.

A large church did a survey of its congregational life which included a detailed analysis of the patterns of giving. One interesting fact they uncovered was that pensioners in that church were the only age group in the church where, as a whole age group, they were giving more than ten per cent of their income to the church. They obviously felt that they belonged.

Another interesting fact was that leaders (of any sort of group, project, or activity in the church) gave twice as much as members of the groups they ran. Again, people's giving of money was related to the extent that they had invested themselves and their efforts into the life and work of the church.

Finding ways to help church members let these factors – *grace, vision/ vocation,* and *belonging* – be the motivation of their giving, not just of money, in the whole of life will enrich the life and resources of any church.

The marks of Christian giving

It is important to identify the distinctive and distinguishing marks of Christian giving. This does not mean that all these marks are only expressed by Christian people, but rather they are marks that a Christian community would want to give expression to in the whole of its life, not just in the matter of financial giving.

Relational – a response to love

Though Christian giving is always 'for' something, whether the church or some 'good cause', ultimately it is to God. One of its great distinguishing marks is that, at heart, it is a *response to God – a response to love.*

'We love because he first loved us.' We give, in the first place, to God. Christian giving is rightly an act of worship; moreover, it is not just part of our worship, it is part of our whole-life response to the generosity and goodness of God. This is where vocation is so vital. When people are active in the church not out of moral pressure, but from a sense of call, what they contribute takes on the 'overflowing' mark of the response of love rather than duty.

Generous

Because Christian giving is personal, giving to God, it is furthest from a tax and closest to a gift to a loved one. That means it is approached from the perspective of 'How much can I give?' rather than 'How little can I get away with giving?'. This is where we need to be careful of using tithing as a model. It is significant that, when teaching about giving, neither Jesus (Matthew 6.1–4) nor Paul (2 Corinthians 8, 9) made any reference to tithing as a guiding principle for doing so. Yes, a percentage is a helpful guideline, but all too easily it takes us into a 'tax' and an 'ought' mentality, and robs the act of giving of its fundamental nature as a response of love to love. It is thanksgiving, not paying our dues.

> If ethical duty requires that we give ten per cent of our money away, then love will always look to give more than this. In this way love fulfils the *teleo* (goal) of ethics by existing as the excess of ethics ... A love that is born from God is a love that gives with the same reflex as that which causes a bird to sing or the heart to beat.[5]

Certainly for the Macedonians it was an overflow of love. The more precise translation of the text 'God loves a cheerful giver' is 'God loves an hilarious giver'. It could be said that the Christian is the only person who laughs all the way *from* the bank! However, remember this is not just about money, it is about our whole approach to life. It flows from an *abundance* mentality based on God's overflowing generosity to us rather than a *poverty* mentality. 'Their abundant joy and their extreme poverty have overflowed in a wealth of generosity' (2 Corinthians 8.2).

Freely given

Because Christian giving is a response to love, rather than a tax or even a moral duty, it is freely chosen giving: 'They voluntarily gave according to their means, and even beyond their means, begging us earnestly for the privilege of sharing in this ministry to the saints' (2 Corinthians 8.3).

An incumbent told me once that all he seemed to do about giving in his church, where people gave generously, was to encourage people *not* to give. One member of the church had recently been released from prison after serving a sentence for embezzlement. He was still paying off his creditors but said he wanted to slow that pace down so he could give to the church from which he had received so much loving care. The vicar urged him to clear his debts first. Another member of the church was a non-working housewife whose husband was hostile to the faith and told her he did not want her to give any of the housekeeping to 'that church'. Again, the vicar persuaded her not to. He told both of them that their *desire* to give was what delighted God. They should see the fact that they did *not* give was itself a pleasing sacrifice offered to God. His actions remind us that, in seeking to stimulate the Church's generosity in its financial giving, that we need to be sensitive to, and affirmative of, those who really are called of God *not* to give – doing just that is the offering pleasing to God.

Self-giving

The Incarnation, ministry and passion of Christ are the essential template for Christian giving, well expressed by what Paul saw in the giving of the Macedonian church: 'begging us earnestly for the privilege of sharing in this ministry to the saints – and this, not merely as we expected; they gave themselves first to the Lord and, by the will of God, to us' (2 Corinthians 8.4–6). Too easily, in secular fundraising, the unacknowledged goal is to substitute our money for ourselves.

Ann Morisy, in *Journeying Out*,[6] tells the following story:

> At a Mothers' Union meeting in a village in Kent, the speakers were three Mothers' Union workers from Zimbabwe. In their presentation they spoke about how important hand sewing machines were to the villages in Zimbabwe where there was no electricity. The word went round and soon there were eight old sewing machines retrieved from people's lofts and cellars. However, the Zimbabwean women advised that the only way they could reliably reach the villages would be if they were delivered personally.
>
> The British women, all over 60, were faced with a challenge – would they organize a few jumble sales to pay the shipping costs only to have the machines moulder in a

customs yard, or would they go to Zimbabwe themselves and carry the sewing machines to the villages? Would they choose venturesome love[7] or would they opt for what, in theological terms, Bonhoeffer would have described as cheap grace?

They chose to go to Zimbabwe.

A priestly ministry

One of the distinctives of the ordained ministry is the authority to bless others in the name of God. Peter describes the whole people of God as a Royal Priesthood: something that has been explored earlier (Chapter 2). Ann Morisy, in writing about the above Mother's Union story, does not use *blessing* language but rather the allied image of *cascades of grace* which flowed from the courageous decision to give themselves in this task. She lists the cascade in the following ways:

■ The local newspaper followed the women's story at every stage, carrying the implicit message that church involvement does not have to be dull and predictable.

■ The families of the women hotly debated whether their mothers were being reckless in taking such risks … especially with their bad backs. The grandchildren, however, thought that their grandmothers were *cool*.

■ Prayer became passionate.

■ An understanding of world development issues grew.

■ The women were transformed by their experience – and were radicalized and sensitized by the experience.

■ An ongoing relationship was created between villagers in Zimbabwe and villagers in Kent.

These were only the immediate gracious outcomes.

To participate in self-giving generosity blesses others. It also blesses, and changes us. God is at work in such giving.

Structures for Christian giving

The Resources section at the end of this book has a suggested structure for the annual, prayerful review of personal giving expressed by the completion and handing in of a Pledge Card. While some form of pledging is used quite widely, what is being advocated here is that it is done *annually*, that *everyone* is encouraged to complete a pledge, whether they are changing the level of their giving or not, and that it is developed as a *prayerful and spiritual* expression of discipleship, rather than as simply an efficient approach to 'financial management' in the church. This approach is used by a number of churches that have adopted it, with good results. For example, one church that started this approach in 2010, soon after the Coalition Government's first austerity budget, saw an increase in giving for the following year of over 13 per cent, followed by a further increase of 5 per cent in the year after. When this sort of approach is taken, it really is important to give clear feedback to the church about the level of pledges and the numbers involved. In many churches the number of those involved increases for several years after the initial introduction, as it becomes part of the habit and culture of the church.

No doubt no one structure can fit every situation exactly. Nonetheless, it can equally easily be adapted. However, some of the key characteristics that do need to find a place in any such approach are as follows. The whole process should be set in the context of *prayer*. This involves getting people to give *prayerful consideration* as to what God might be calling them to do about their giving in the coming year. People should be invited to fill in a *pledge form* (with assurance that only the Treasurer and/or Gift Aid Officer will know who gives, or what they give). This is best expressed by holding a Day of Pledging, often called a Thanksgiving Day,[8] during which Pledge Cards (in sealed envelopes) are brought forward in a special *act of giving*. Most churches which take this approach do encourage everyone to complete a pledge even if their giving is unchanged. In this way the church has some assurance about the likely future level of giving.

> Three times during my 22-year incumbency the giving level dropped from what it had been the previous year. We learned an important lesson through these 'shocks'. Basically such a drop was usually one of the first signs that all was not well in the life of the church. People withdraw giving before they withdraw their presence. Frankly, my instinct was to berate the church for its poor level of giving, but wiser heads around me got us to listen to the church and to God about what 'dis-ease' in the church this was highlighting. Each time we uncovered some malaise. Once the issue had been addressed, the giving continued to grow. It is a reminder of the inter-connectedness of church life.

Particularly where churches are introducing the Pledging approach outlined in this chapter, it is important not only to report levels of giving after each

Pledging Day, but also to keep the church regularly informed (in an easily accessible way) about how the money given is being used and what are the particular pressure points on the church in the area of its finances at present. This keeps 'givers' and 'spenders' in good communication with each other.

The place for fundraising

The distinction between Christian giving and a fundraising mentality with which this chapter opened, primarily concerned two contrasting mindsets. However, it needs to be noted and acknowledged that there are situations where a combination of the two approaches is needed. There are small rural and deprived inner-city churches whose buildings require funding that no amount of Christian giving can address. For example, an inner-city parish with 80 worshippers, half of whom are retired and only 15 of the rest are in full-time employment, needs to raise over two million pounds to build a hall for community activities alongside the church and to do necessary re-ordering of the worship area itself. This sort of situation is quite widespread. Here, what still matters is the mindset of the church. Is it committed to Christian giving as God's call, with a recognition that fundraising and the seeking of grants will also be necessary? Or, is its first priority getting others to pay so that the church does not need to address its part? That is the real issue, and in many such situations such generosity is evident. Moreover, it is that generosity that moves others to make up for what is lacking. So while the two mentalities fight each other, the two elements, Christian giving and seeking of grants, can work well together.

Conclusion

Finances, and the associated anxiety about them, can dominate the life of clergy and the agendas of Church Councils. When that happens it is vital for the church to come to the situation with faith and with actions founded on good theology rather than secular thinking. Churches that fail to do so sometimes end up having to pay a heavy price. If a secular 'fundraising' mentality takes hold, the whole life of the church can be dominated by fundraising events. Congregations grow weary with an endless round of such activities and the spiritual priorities of the church get pushed into the background. This debilitates the life of the church and causes people to give up taking part in such events or even in participating in the life of the church. Their withdrawal adds to the problems and then church life gets sucked into a vicious spiral of increased activity producing ever-diminishing returns.

The good news is that this does not have to happen and there are ways through. A very different dynamic can be at work. Where giving, and all forms of service, are encouraged and developed on the basis of godly motivation and in response to the call of God, then the handling of money can reinforce the church's spiritual life. Then a vicious spiral is replaced by a virtuous spiral that takes a church up to a new level of awareness of and appreciation for the goodness, generosity and greatness of God. Such a church, in the whole of its life, then becomes a powerful witness to the goodness of God to the world around – usually without any attempt to draw attention to its self or its giving.

It has been noted above that the secular and Christian approaches to giving often exist alongside each other. It is usually best, when seeking to develop the Christian approach, to look for ways of reducing the 'fundraising' focus. Churches can find, however, that when the 'fundraising' element is taken out of events such as summer garden parties and autumn fairs there is still a longing for such events. This is usually because they are primarily *social* events. That is great and is a good reason for retaining the events. This may be without any financial element. However, the Christian giving emphasis can be introduced by retaining the fundraising element but directing it outwards to needs in the local community and further afield.

The path to the positive and godly spiral, as set out in this chapter, is challenging, but it is also life-giving and faith-building. Taking this path, which needs to be done consistently over the years, results in churches *being* good news, not just *having* good news to tell others.

For further help see *Part 3: Resources*, 'Introduction', pp. 137–9, 'Study questions', pp. 168–70, and 'Leaders' resources', p. 181 and pp. 190–3.

Chapter 9
Re-working evangelism

Much of what has been said and done in the realm of mission, in recent years, has been an intuitive response to the changes in today's culture. There is plenty that is good in that response, but we do also need to think through what we are saying and doing in order to ensure that the church's mission is built on solid foundations.

There has also been plenty of confusion in the use of the terms 'mission' and 'evangelism' that needs addressing. So the first step in re-thinking, and then re-working, mission and evangelism is to define our terms clearly. Doing so has the benefit also of putting mission and evangelism in the context of what has been explored so far.

Defining our terms

The terms 'mission' and 'evangelism' are often used interchangeably. Particularly is this so in the evangelical tradition. The tendency to put the two words together reveals, subconsciously, the view that evangelism is the *real* work. So mission is evangelism and evangelism is mission. In this view the goal of 'mission' is simply personal conversion. All the associated work of mission is a means to this end. In the liberal tradition the terms are often used the other way round so that the *real* work becomes caring for the whole person, not least in their physical circumstances, which is virtually equated with evangelism.

That summary is a caricature of those two traditions; in both of them there is a considerable range and emphases, and churches in both traditions have come to a much more integrated understanding of these elements. Yet these overall views need to be recognized and addressed, for they are fairly widespread.

It is good for churches of all traditions to consider how one aspect of the mission of the church relates to another, and this can helpfully be done by defining a number of terms. These key terms are set out, in summary form, in the box below. There is a logical sequence about the order. The following comments fill out these single-sentence summaries, as follows.

Kingdom: God's action in bringing humanity and all creation to its intended fulfilment in Christ.

Mission: sharing in God's loving purposes for the wholeness of humanity and all creation.

Evangelism: the processes whereby people become disciples of Jesus Christ.

Spirituality: how encounter with God is experienced, expressed and nurtured.

Church: lived embodiment and outworking of *mission, evangelism* and *spirituality.*

The kingdom

The kingdom is the dominant theme of the teaching of Jesus, yet churches struggle to grasp its relevance to their work. It can be a rather elusive term. It is striking how rarely it is mentioned in church Mission Action Plans. Yet this was both the mission and the gospel in the teaching of Jesus.

> Now after John was arrested, Jesus came to Galilee, proclaiming the good news of the kingdom of God, and saying, 'The time is fulfilled, and the kingdom of God has come near; repent, and believe in the good news.' (Mark 1.15)

> Soon afterwards he went through cities and villages, proclaiming and bringing the good news of the kingdom of God. (Luke 8.1)

> These twelve Jesus sent out with the following instructions '... As you go, proclaim the good news, "The kingdom of heaven has come near."' (Matthew 10.5–7)

This is the heart of the message of Jesus. The 'kingdom', or 'sphere of divine rule' describes God's overall purposes in his world. It is about bringing heaven upon earth. Hence: 'Your kingdom come, your will be done on earth as it is in heaven' (Matthew 6.10). Another way of seeing this is about the future (heaven) breaking into the here and now of broken humanity. This kingdom is bigger than the Church. It is about God's care for, and purposes of love towards, all humanity, indeed, all creation.

In the history of the Church the kingdom has often been shifted into 'eternity' mode by being considered the state of bliss in which the saints live – heaven. The teaching of Christ makes it clear that something more immediate is at work now. The term 'eternal life' really means 'the life of the new age' or 'the life of the world to come'. As Christians we are called to live *now* by the values of the *age to come*.

A classic expression of this vision of a new order of reality can be seen in the life and ministry of Archbishop Desmund Tutu with his vision of a 'rainbow people'. The image is in such striking contrast to the 'black and white' mindset of apartheid. Within the vision of a new order of reality, he saw – and worked tirelessly for – the Church to be a 'rainbow people of God', a sign of the new order towards which the Spirit of God was leading the whole nation.

Cecily Saunders' development of the hospice movement is another example of the kingdom dynamic at work. Here was someone saying, in effect, that there must be a better way of caring for the dying. The very use of the term 'hospice' was intended to show that something is being done here which comes at the issue from a different perspective.

These, and countless other initiatives, arose from people of faith who had a vision of 'another country ... whose ways are ways of gentleness and all her paths are peace'. The kingdom is the backdrop and context in which all of God's purposes are to be seen.

Mission

This is the outworking of the kingdom dynamic in particular situations. We have David Bosch[1] to thank for drawing the Church's attention to the fact that, for the first 1,800 years of the Church's life, 'mission' was understood as what *God* does ('God so loved the world that he gave ...'). Only in the last few centuries has it been used to mean what the *Church* does. Mission is, then, the outworking of God's purposes of love for humanity and all creation. The initiative is God's; yet too often the Church has seen mission more like something we are doing for God – keeping the family business going. So Bosch says:

> Mission is ... the good news of God's love, incarnated in the witness of a community, for the sake of the world.

and

> To participate in mission is to participate in the movement of God's love towards people, since God is a fountain of sending love.

If mission is what God is doing in bringing in his kingdom, then all attempts by the Church to 'engage in mission' must begin with God. It must involve the discerning of what God is wanting done, or what God is already at work doing, which draws us into his work. This is why 'vocation' is crucial to our participation in God's mission. We need to discover what and how and why God might be calling us to engage in the coming of his kingdom.

However, a health warning is appropriate here. We cannot necessarily (or, even, ever) know in a defined way the end result of the coming of God's kingdom, because the kingdom is not a programme but a dynamic reality at work in the world.

> When the Revd Chad Varah set up his 'Samaritans telephone ministry' in a London parish he had no idea that it would lead to a worldwide network of similar agencies that now, at any time of day or night, has tens of thousands of people on the end of a telephone ready to talk with those who are feeling desperate.

So mission comes from God's initiative rather than ours; which is why prayer and spirituality are so integral to its functioning.

Evangelism

This is rightly understood as an aspect of the wider work of mission. It has been helpfully defined as 'the processes whereby people become disciples of Jesus Christ'. For its health, evangelism is best set within the wider vision of mission. True, it is quite valid for evangelism to be done as a distinct activity, as in an 'evangelistic service' or through the running of courses (such as Alpha, Emmaus, Start and many others). However, the more mission and evangelism are held together, the better. Once they become too separated, evangelism is liable to lapse into a membership recruitment drive, and mission into social work. Indeed, it is best if evangelism is put in the context of the kingdom and mission. Then it becomes *an invitation* (evangelism) to join in with what God is doing in the world (mission).

Spirituality

This has already been explored in previous chapters, but because of the interaction of mission and evangelism, it needs to shape both. Mission is discerned out of our spirituality and through our response to the call of God (vocation). Evangelism is the conscious passing on of that spirituality, explaining our experience of the 'Up', 'In' and 'Out' dimensions of knowing God and how others can come into an experience of God that draws them into that same dynamic relationship with God.

Church

Within the flow of these terms it is vital to include the Church, for it enables us to see that the primary nature of the Church is not a building, or even an organization or institution. The Church is a community called into being by God (*ecclesia* = the called-out people) to be a lived demonstration of the kingdom of God. The Church is a pilot project for the coming of that kingdom, a sphere where God's rule shapes attitudes, actions, values, priorities and agendas. The Church is a community gathered around Jesus Christ in such a way that it gives flesh to the Christian gospel, embodying the outworking of mission, evangelism and spirituality. Its calling is to be a lived demonstration of the knowledge of God: truth incarnate.

Trends in evangelism

There have been many subtle yet substantial changes in the way in which the Church engages in the work of evangelism that are spelt out below. It is good to note these trends for it helps us spot where, and why, and how best to develop and nurture it in the local church.

One of the primary shifts has been *from event to process*. Whereas, traditionally, the Church sought to do the work of evangelism by holding 'Missions', of which the Billy Graham missions were a classic example, today the approach is very different. Now the emphasis is on inviting people to groups where the Christian faith is explored and where people can talk about it. Such groups last from four or five to ten or more sessions. Evangelism is done as part of a sustained *process*. The setting is informal, and there is a mix of believers and enquirers, so that those 'enquiring' not only have opportunity to gather information about the Christian faith, and an opportunity to voice doubts, objections and contrary perceptions, but also can observe the faith being demonstrated by the group with whom they are meeting.

One of the biggest problems for many churches is that there are not enough 'enquirers' to form such a group. One way is to look for people who might have the skill to visit people in their homes to do a one-to-one 'course' with those interested.

Another approach, taken by a number of churches, is often called a 'Food for Thought' event. Typically a church, or village hall, is used to lay on a good quality meal at low cost (subsidized) with an invitation to come and hear some speaker on the subject of 'my work and my faith'. This takes the form of an after-dinner speech at the end of which people are informed of a new 'exploring the faith group' starting in two weeks' time (typically for five or six sessions) to which people can sign up at the end of the evening.

This 'Food for Thought', approach was first done in a rural church and it remains one of the most effective and achievable ways of doing evangelism in the rural context.

A further significant trend is *from gifted individual to priestly community*. Evangelists, whether big name ones, or simply church members, have often been seen as gifted solo performers or even oddities. However, much evangelism today is actually taking place through the church as an embodiment of the faith.

> # The second mark of a healthy church:
>
> ## has an outward looking focus

The Reformers were not at their best in introducing the concept of 'the priesthood of all believers'. Working against the background of a 'priest-ridden' practice of the Church, it is understandable that they should want to emphasize the 'priestly nature' of all believers. However, the scriptures never use the phrase 'the priesthood of all believers'. But they do talk about the Church being a 'royal priesthood'. In that phrase, 'priesthood' is a collective noun; it describes a community. So, for example, in a church of 50 worshippers, it is not so much that there are 50 priests, as that there is one – the believing community.

Now the role of priest is to act as a communicator between God and humanity: praying to God for the people and blessing the people in the name of God. This is the fundamental role of the Christian community – to bless the community around it, in the name of God. This is not about *pronouncing* a blessing but *being* a blessing. When a church functions like that, evangelism takes place as part of the whole. The story with which this chapter ends illustrates this life-giving dynamic of a loving community communicating the knowledge of God in action.

Using the 'Up', 'In' and 'Out' framework, in a carefully thought through, well-planned and intentional way, a church becomes a priestly community in practice when each of those dimensions is functioning well. This happens when someone encounters God as the church focuses on God (worship), or when it practises a quality of loving attention in its network of relationships (community), or when people are touched by its service to the wider world (mission). This is the ultimate calling of the church – to be a royal priesthood that points to the reality and goodness of God by the way it functions and by what it does. When that happens, as we shall see in Chapter 10, mission and evangelism flow together as a stream from the very throne of God to an often parched land around.

It is worth noting that such an approach to evangelism is good news for churches, and particularly rural churches, that have small numbers. This sort of holistic evangelism arises out of our *being* much more than out of our *doing*.

Another important trend is the shift *from doctrine to spirituality*. This does not, or should not, mean the abandonment of doctrine, but rather of taking spirituality as the starting point. Nonetheless, we need to heed the warning that:

> Many of us begin our faith with an encounter and end with nothing but a doctrine.[2]

There is a widespread interest in spirituality today and it is good to connect with this by offering people access to an exploration of the Christian faith from the perspective of Christian spirituality. Apart from any other advantages, most church members are more comfortable in talking about how they relate to God, not least in prayer and worship. This is often how conversations develop. Moreover, in seeking to return to the heart of what the faith is all about, namely the knowledge of God, the church should be in the business of developing the spiritual life of its members which, in itself, will equip them to answer questions from others about how a relationship with God works.

> **One church ran a series of Quiet Days for church members. The last hour of each day was focused on 'How might we talk about our relationship with God to those who are seeking after God/something?' This included asking members of the group beforehand what questions they had been asked by such people, as well as by gleaning from websites, conversations and articles the sort of questions people are looking for an answer to.**

Linked to this is the trend to shift *from speaking to listening*. That is, rather than the church starting by telling others what we believe, churches start by asking others to tell us about their own spiritual searchings and longings. Jesus took this approach on the road to Emmaus, asking the two disciples, 'What are you discussing with each other while you walk along?' (Luke 24.17).

One church took this approach seriously (working on the principle that people are 'hard-wired for spirituality') and put a major focus (equivalent to the emphasis on Christian distinctives set out in Chapter 4 above) on helping people to listen, deeply, to others. This included listening to the unspoken longings, searchings and 'aspirations' of others. They then went on to develop a series of questions with these church members that might give people an opening to talk about 'the spiritual dimension of life'. These questions included 'Have you ever had a spiritual experience?', and 'Have you ever had a sense of God answering your prayers?', and 'Have you ever been aware of God being present with you?' What they found was twice as much as they had expected. First, they found people eager to talk about their own spiritual and religious experiences. Second, they discovered that this had the effect of provoking those they talked to, off their own initiative, wanting to explore further those occasional experiences that they had been reminded of by those sort of conversations.

Other churches have used material that explores ways of relating faith to modern life through the use of modern films. *Chocolat* is a favourite such film. Websites such as 'Reel Faith: where meaning meets the movies' have plenty of good resources to this end.

Some churches using the Catechumenate (literally 'teaching process') approach gather groups together and invite them to set their agenda of the questions they want to find answers to. Some then go on to invite anyone in the group to introduce a session on their chosen theme. This gives the incumbent, or group leader, the opportunity to help people discover resources, including 'faith resources', that could be helpful in their running such a session. People are empowered by this sort of approach, though it does require nerve and skill to make it work.

The accompanied journey

There is a particular significance in the link between *spirituality* and *listening* that may well prove vital for the further development of evangelism. It is beautifully expressed in the ministry of Christ on the road to Emmaus. If I may put it like this, it would have been understandable if Jesus had called out to the two disciples and said something along the lines 'Hi, folks, it's me, Jesus. I have risen from the dead!'

I jest, yet it draws attention to the striking way in which he did handle the situation; not by talking about or exploring his own experience (arguably the most striking 'spiritual experience' in all human history), but by asking about their recent experiences. 'What are you discussing with each other while you walk along?' (Luke 24.17). His focus was on their 'spiritual experience', and questionings, not on his.

Mark Yaconelli suggests that there are three phases in this approach which are covered in the last three chapters of his book, namely, *noticing*, *naming* and *nurturing*. As a youth pastor, quoted by him, puts it:

> I think the most powerful aspect of contemplative youth min-
> istry has been giving young people the space and opportunity
> to notice God in their lives. Creating exercises where kids can
> notice God invites a sense of wonder.[3]

This does not just apply to youth work but to all engagement with those not yet aware of a relationship with God in Christ. The starting point needs to be with their experience. Now, where a church is nurturing the spirituality of its members, and – not least as part of that – developing people's listening skills, it is well placed to engage in such work. Indeed, it is likely to be doing that quite instinctively, even if it does not occur to them to see it as evangelism.

Maybe the best help churches can give their members is to enable them to take people on a *noticing–naming–nurturing* journey when they start to share stories such as this one from a *Times* newspaper columnist:[4]

> Just before Christmas, lugging John Lewis bags down Ox-
> ford Street, Central London, I took a phone call containing
> grim news. Suddenly the garish stores and clamour of shop-
> pers were physically unbearable. I had to be quiet and alone.
> Stumbling on through the crowds, I came to a church, which
> I assumed, given the spate of London metal thefts, would be
> locked. Luckily, although deserted, it was open.

> I threw down my bags and sat for a long while. A lifelong non-
> believer, a former rowdy teenage atheist, I drank in the peace
> and left restored.

> This, I discovered later, was St Giles-in-the-Fields, known as
> the Poets' Church, since it is where Milton, Byron and Shelley
> had their children baptized and where Marvell is buried; writers
> who evoke the joy of both earthly experience and the divine.

It struck me then that while intellectually I am on the side of Richard Dawkins, facing down the bigotry and illogic of belief, mindful of all religious intrusion into the secular political sphere, my soul has needs that science cannot address.

Where would the atheist firebrands have me go to feel sad, to reflect upon loss and the savage unrelenting passage of time? A science museum maybe; an art gallery; a psychotherapist's couch; under a night sky, marvelling at the infinity of the cosmos? All have their appeal, but none would have that church's mystery.

Mystery is something I never thought I would need.

As discussed earlier, in dealing with pastoral care, mutuality is vital here. Telling someone the answers is not the first priority. Initially the task is to share with such a person in exploring the nature of the mystery we long for. So, for us today, we need to take other people's spiritual experience and our calling to listen deeply, in a really serious way, and to trust God with the journey that might open up for either of us.

The reality of the situation

The fact is that, for many churches, evangelism is a pressing need as ageing congregations face the truth that their church could be in terminal decline. New people are not joining the church, other than a few 'incomers' who have moved house. If the situation continues, the church will close before long. The recruitment of new members is essential for the survival of the church.

However, the problem is that evangelism motivated by church survival is, at best, a defective motive, and could well actually be counter-productive, as David Runcorn argues:

> The very factors that are jolting us into missionary mode – numerical decline and financial crisis – are not, in themselves, Christian motives for mission. In fact they may easily distort both motive and method. But it is not primarily strategies or structures we need so much as a transformation of consciousness. We need a new way of seeing and imagining.[5]

Moreover:

When so much needs to happen outwardly and visibly there is real pressure to neglect the hard, steady work of putting down deep roots for our living and praying.

This is the course that has been argued for in previous chapters; that what is needed is a return to the heart of what faith is all about, namely the knowledge of God. The need of the hour is for a renewal and re-working of the inner spiritual dynamic of the Church. Doing this will require that we draw upon the riches of our Christian heritage, not abandon them (see Chapter 3).

Just as the pursuit of happiness for its own sake rarely produces happiness, so a membership recruitment drive is unlikely to produce new followers of Jesus Christ. In considering how giving might be re-worked we looked at the renewal of the heart of Christian giving, not getting others to fund our activities. So here, in the matter of evangelism, though new members are important, our focus needs to be one of renewing the inner spiritual dynamic of the church community and its members. When it comes to the sharing of faith it is, again, *listening* that needs to be our starting point.

The greater reality

Tough though our setting is, today's fragmented culture creates fissures in which the precious seeds of the love of God can take root. This is most likely to happen where a healthy church is nurturing the spirituality and sense of vocation and thanksgiving that arise out of faith in Christ. When that happens, we gain glimpses of the wonder of the grace of God in action in practical service issuing in the passing on of the faith.

> One of the most moving moments in my 22-year incumbency was when a couple, who were not members of any church, arranged to see me because they wanted to ask a favour of me. Not knowing them, I had no idea what they would want. If I had known them, I am not sure I could have guessed either!
>
> They said that although not churchgoers and not sure what they believed (but it was changing, as this story tells why), the favour they wanted was permission to come to one of our services and say a public 'Thank you' to God and the members of the church who had helped them recently. They then related their story, of which I had known nothing until they told me.

The husband was required by his work to attend a three-day conference in Germany. The couple decided to book in to a local hotel and then stay on for a few more days. In the midst of this programme, the wife went into premature labour, was rushed to hospital and their child was born: stillborn. Naturally they were distraught; more so because, not knowing any German, they were not able to communicate to the hospital authorities that they wished to take the body of the child home for burial in England.

They soon realized that they needed help but were not sure who to turn to. In desperation the wife rang the leader of the parent and toddler group in the parish, with whom she had struck up a good relationship, and poured out her troubles to her. She was not particularly looking for help, just someone to share her troubles with. This was on a Sunday evening. The group leader arranged to ring them back first thing on the Monday to let them know if they thought they could be of any help or give them any advice.

On the Monday morning the group leader reported that she had been in contact with other members of the leadership team with the following results. They had found a member of the group who was German speaking and willing to fly out that day to be with them and help them in their negotiations. The group had also contributed enough funds for this person's air fare and hotel costs. They were now at the airport and expected to be with them before lunch that day.

They duly arrived, helped negotiate with the hospital authorities and arranged for the body to be flown back to England.

Would I be willing to do them the favour of publicly standing up in church to say 'Thank you' to the people who had helped and to the God (whom they rather thought they now believed in!) who had inspired such a response?

It was a moving and humbling experience of overflowing generosity, self-giving and sacrificial love that remains with me today as an inspiration of what can happen if God's people dare to be open to divine promptings and dare to act in 'venturesome love' that not only meets needs but brings the presence of God into places of human pain. My part, as vicar, in all this was simply to say 'Yes – do come and give thanks to God and to those through whom he has shown you something of the reality of his love!' It proved to be all part of their journey into the knowledge of God.

True mission, inspired by an openness to the grace and call of God, overflows with such generosity of love that the gospel is proclaimed so clearly in the deeds that few words are needed. Those words are to name the experience and its connection with God.

For further help see *Part 3: Resources*, 'Introduction', pp. 137–9, 'Study questions', pp. 171–6, and 'Leaders' resources', p. 181 and pp. 194–6.

Chapter 10
Re-working mission

There are few areas in the life of the Church where 'silo', or compartmentalized, thinking[1] is more evident than in its engagement in mission. Typically, a church might run a luncheon club for the elderly or a parent and toddler or nursery group, but all its thinking and planning are within the mindset and worldview of a secular, social services, perspective. Ann Morisy writes of 'the danger of secularizing the Church from within'.[2]

Such an approach only makes sense if we consider that our faith has nothing distinctive to contribute to the way we seek to serve others. Yet, are there really no distinguishing marks about how such work is done (other than possibly charging less for our services) compared to the secular world? If there is nothing distinctive in our engagement with the world around us, that might explain the disappointment that is often voiced about the lack of 'response' from the local community. Some are puzzled as to why the Church has built so many bridges into the community, yet very few make the journey to faith across those bridges. Could it be that so little spirituality is going out that very little faith is coming back?

This chapter explores how we might re-connect mission with the knowledge of God and how the church can express the distinctive aspects of its service of others. In doing so, this will, necessarily, engage with both the obstacles to our doing so and also the rich heritage we have to draw on as we seek to engage in God's loving purposes for all.

> **Kingdom:** God's action in bringing humanity and all creation to its intended fulfilment in Christ.
>
> **Mission**: sharing in God's loving purposes for the wholeness of humanity and all creation.
>
> **Evangelism**: the processes whereby people become disciples of Jesus Christ.
>
> **Spirituality**: how encounter with God is experienced, expressed and nurtured.
>
> **Church**: lived embodiment and outworking of *mission, evangelism* and *spirituality*.

This earlier set of definitions is repeated here as an essential starting point for our understanding of what mission is all about. It is the outworking of the knowledge of God (spirituality) in and through the life of a faith community (church) so as to join in with the purposes of God (kingdom) in giving loving attention to the needs of the world around us (mission), drawing people to the fire of God's love (evangelism) so that they may share with us in God's life-giving mission to all creation.

However, there is an important preliminary we need to look at concerning the scope and focus of Christian mission. It introduces us to the bigger picture of where such mission finds expression.

The bigger picture

When we think about the local church engaging in mission, we almost invariably limit our thinking to organizations the church has set up to serve the local community. The fact that we do so is further evidence of the extent to which we instinctively think of the church in organizational terms. However, that is not the limit of mission, nor is it necessarily the most important aspect of the church's mission. One way of seeing the fuller extent of mission is by considering the following three modes of local church mission.

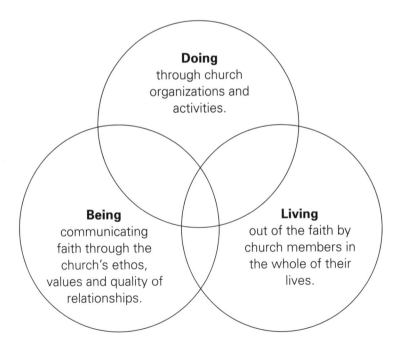

Doing
through church organizations and activities.

Being
communicating faith through the church's ethos, values and quality of relationships.

Living
out of the faith by church members in the whole of their lives.

The 'Doing' mode

This is the most obvious and visible part of mission. It involves running groups, typically focused on age groups such as toddlers, after-school club, youth groups, OAP luncheon clubs, as well as single-sex groups such as the Mothers' Union or men's groups. Also, to be included in this mode, is the hiring out of halls to other groups for them to run activities. These can be important ways of engaging in mission, though it is vital to remember the dictum that 'It's not what you do but the way that you do it.' These organizations *can be* great expressions of the love of God incarnate in human care. But they can also reflect little, if anything, of the good news. It depends how far spirituality has led to true community and on into sharing the work of the compassion of Christ.

Moreover, particularly smaller, often rural churches may be richly involved in Christian mission without setting up a single organization.

> A recent survey of volunteers discovered that regular church worshippers are 70 per cent *more* likely to be involved in voluntary community work than those who are not regular worshippers.[3]

Not only do they not have the resources to run things such as luncheon clubs for the elderly, but it would be counter-productive to do so. Their role, rather, is to join in with the village groups running such activities. In these situations the church is not called to be *light* (with its own visible structures) but rather *leaven* (hidden within local activities). However, this call to be leaven is not just 'a nice picture', it is a serious piece of work. It may well mean that church members involved in these activities need to meet together to reflect on their calling in this setting, to pray for the work and to discern together how best to make a creative, godly contribution to what is being done and the way it is being conducted. The later section on 'Mission as living the Christian distinctives' might well form a useful basis for such prayer and reflection, together with engaging with any, or all, of the four books on mission noted in the Resources section (p. 179).

The 'Being' mode

We are familiar with the saying, 'What you are shouts so loud that I cannot hear what you say.' The 'Being' mode is about this 'what you are'. It is where the 'Up' to God, 'In' to others and 'Out' to the world around us are being effectively expressed. It should mean that anyone experiencing the church's worship, its community and relational life, and its service of others, experiences something of the reality of the knowledge of God. It will also include physical things such as the state of the church grounds, noticeboards and buildings, but goes beyond that to the attitude of people to newcomers of any sort. Are non-members attracted or frozen out by our attitude to them? More importantly, do those making initial contact with the church get any sense of generous welcome, of people putting themselves out to help, and of a spiritual dimension to what is going on here?

Here are three contrasting stories.

> A single senior citizen man came to a church service for the first time. He was a member of the local community and part of a singing group whom a number of people in the choir knew. The only people who spoke to him after the service were three members of the choir who, separately, all pleaded with him to join the choir. No one asked him why he was there, said how good it was to see him, or showed interest in anything other than his making up the numbers. He did not return.

> An elderly woman went to church for the first time. The churchwarden greeted her warmly and shook her hand, whereupon she burst into tears. They sat her down and got her a drink of water. By this time they had two distressed people, the visiting woman and the churchwarden who was wondering what he had done wrong. Eventually the woman had collected herself sufficiently to turn to the churchwarden and say, 'You are the first person to touch me for three years.' She went on to become a member of that church and be part of the network of relationships there.

> A single mother had recently moved far from her home town after the painful breakup of her marriage. She was not a churchgoer but thought she might 'give it a try' and see what it was like and find out 'what church is all about'. She, with her two children, felt nervous when they first went but were given a good welcome. It was helpful in practical ways, for example they were given the right books for the service and were taken to sit with someone who related well to them. They quickly felt accepted and 'part of the church'. However, they were neither quickly recruited into jobs needing to be done, nor pressurized about their faith, their giving or anything else. When she had settled (after the best part of a year) and through friends with a few other young mothers, she went to a group exploring the faith.

She was deeply touched by the way the course was handled and its content, and knew at the end of it that, despite
a deep sense of failure, she was loved by God. Within two
years she was leading a group befriending other single
mothers in the community.

Her journey had passed seamlessly through the experience of a quality
of relationships ('In' to one another), on to a personal encounter with
God ('Up' to God) and through into service of others ('Out' to the world
around). Here the faith is at work. A healthy church is reflecting something
of the love of God to others.

The 'Living' mode

The Christian faith is 'not just for Christmas' and 'not just for Sunday'.
It is not so much a religion as a way of life; called, in its earliest days,
simply 'The Way'. Yet the faith can easily be constrained within a churchy
framework. Many years ago a book about the church was written called
God's Frozen People – as distinct from God's *chosen* people.[4] It was
written in the early days of 'every-member ministry' and put lay people
into two categories: 'churchly laity' and 'worldly laity'. The terms are
unflattering and inelegant but they make an important point. There are
some church members who do devote themselves to serving God in and
through the life of the church. However, there are more who are serving
God primarily in the work, social, leisure and political aspects of life. As
Robin Greenwood puts it: 'for the vast majority of laity … the main focus
of their ministry lies in the opportunities presented by their everyday
responsibilities'.[5] It is this aspect that is often seriously neglected in the
life and thinking of the church and its leaders, but there are exceptions.

The clergy in one suburban church became very aware
of how frequently church members in paid employment
spoke negatively about meetings at work, and especially
committee meetings. They decided to do something about
this. They read about how to run good meetings and got
national experts on the subject to speak to members of
the church and to advise them how to run their meetings.
They developed the goal of running all meetings and com-
mittees of the church in life-giving, creative and liberating
ways. This was both an end in itself and also the means to
another end. They wanted to equip as many church members as possible with a rich and regular experience of *good*
meetings and *productive* committee work that they could
take into their work situation in order to be leaven in the
lump of the working environment.

> A church appointed a new vicar. Inevitably those involved
> in the selection were 'inner-core' people. Their goal was
> clear, they wanted someone who could harness the ener-
> gies of the large 'fringe' of the church to help in 'church
> work' and thus take the pressure off the core. Within six
> months of arriving, the new vicar had made an interest-
> ing discovery that led to a costly decision. He realized that
> the 'fringe' were not the ones who were half-hearted about
> their faith. They were actually the more committed believ-
> ers. It was just that they saw their primary calling to express
> that faith in the work and community realms, rather than in
> church. So, in effect, the vicar joined the fringe! Naturally
> the 'core' were appalled at this betrayal of 'their' calling.
> He learned in painful experience the truth of Paul's words
> that 'death is at work in us but life in you'. However, the life
> and faith of the whole church was greatly enhanced by this
> move and exercised a quite striking ministry in a range of
> settings in the local community.

This *living* will, inevitably, mean that members of any particular church are engaged in activities outside the parish and in organizations that are much bigger than the purely local. It is important to keep this bigger picture in mind and find ways to make connection with it in the local setting. One church, in a mining village, managed to go through the whole of the miners' strike in the 1980s without any reference to, or prayer about, what was taking place all around and affecting people's lives deeply. On the positive side, commenting on the part played by various organizations during the foot-and-mouth crisis, Ben Gill (President of the National Farmers' Union), said: 'The only organization that has come out of the crisis well has been the Church.'[6]

When thinking about re-working the mission aspect of the church's life, it is, therefore, vital that we hold all three of these modes in mind, resisting the temptation to think purely in terms of mission as running 'church organizations'. With this richer perspective in mind we can turn now to consider how such mission might be re-worked by giving expression to the distinctives of the Christian faith.

Mission as living the Christian distinctives

Mission is supremely a sphere in which the Christian distinctives are to be expressed. These include the following.

Kingdom vision

The kingdom of God is an expression of both God's *nature* and his *purposes*. It is a living, dynamic reality. A crucial test here is whether our vision is shrinking or growing. We all know how easily a great vision, for example for youth work 'to introduce young people to faith in Christ', can shrink to nothing more than 'keeping the kids off the streets'.

But visions can and do grow as we press on in prayer and service. In such situations we can be rather like Alexander Bell who, when asked how significant for mankind he thought his invention of the telephone might prove to be, replied: 'Very significant. I can imagine the day coming when there will be one of these in every town in America.' Little did he know quite how things would work out. When we set out in mission our vision may be limited, but it does not matter so long as, in the midst of serving, we are also seeking to enter into God's purposes in our service. What matters is that in our praying, planning and reflecting on our work, we hold on to the bigger vision of the coming of God's kingdom rather than simply 'running an activity'.

Holding on to that bigger vision will sometimes involve us in holding fast to our labours over a sustained period. The abolition of slavery cost some their health and their lives and took over forty years. Yet, what a rich fruit their labour bore.

Quality relationships

The two great commandments are about love of God and love of others; this is the heart of mission. It is how we express our love for God and his loving purposes for all. So one of the distinctives in the way mission is expressed should be in the quality of our relationships with others.

> The third mark of a healthy church:
>
> **seeks to find out what God wants**

This is most likely to flourish where those engaging in mission meet regularly to *pray for those they serve* in these ventures, being open to how the Spirit might lead their engagement and seeking to catch a glimpse of God's loving purposes for those with whom we are working.

This will involve a concern for the whole person, not just their physical needs.

> One church group that ran a luncheon club for the elderly met regularly for prayer before they began the preparation work in the kitchen. Their prayer always concluded, not with the normal Grace, but with the Aaronic blessing[7] – for those who would be coming. They had a minute's silence after each line during which, usually in silence, they held, or named before God, members or aspects of the group that came to their attention. This prayer, seemingly for others, doubtless was fulfilled through God inspiring those who took part to be the embodiment of that blessing in their own actions.

Such quality of relationships will be enhanced where those involved have been helped to develop both their ability to *listen* and their *conversation* skills. Doing this not only enriches the lives of those who come to the luncheon club, but also the lives of those 'serving' them. In this way the church was 'growing people'.

> Out of this prayer focus the group running the luncheon club came to see that preparing and serving the meal was not the only task. Relating to those who came was arguably even more important. This led them to increase the size of the team to include cooks and conversationalists; not that these were two distinct groups, though most tended to focus primarily on one of these two roles.

> Later on, conversations led to issues of faith – almost invariably raised by club members – and to the offer of prayer. The club met in a partitioned-off former aisle of the church, so making it easy for people to go into the church and be prayed for. Several came to faith through this informal conversation–relationship–prayer dynamic.

Creativity

Openness to God and others can lead on to our being open to new ways of doing things that are life-enhancing. Prayer, and honest exploring conversations among the leaders, should be sufficient to enable a group to find ways of doing a better job that will be good news for others.

> One of the leaders of a parent and toddler group noticed two different things going on at the same time one day.

The leaders were in the kitchen having 'a good gossip'. Because the kitchen had a long counter that opened into the meeting room where the group was, she saw that most of the parents were coping with children. Those whose children were happily occupied were sitting in silence around the room.

The leaders realized that it would be better if, every week, two or three mothers were invited to help in the kitchen and two or three leaders went into the group to help with the children and to engage the other parents in conversations. In both these ways the parents (usually mothers) got to have adult conversations. Out of this process real relationships of openness and honesty (both ways) developed. Some made the journey to faith through the quality of this work. All this was the fruit of a group of people becoming intentionally relational and mission-focused.

Vocation

This has been explored already[8] but needs to be noted here, for it is vital in two particular ways in the realm of mission.

First, discovering the church's call in the community. Vocation is not just for individuals, it is for communities of faith too. Indeed this is what Mission Action Plans should be all about, to discern God's call for this faith community.[9] It takes time to discern this call, but doing so bears rich fruit. Perhaps the most important thing about this discernment is to recognize and act on the truth that vocation arises from the community. It is not something to be imposed on a church by the leadership.

One church was aware of the number of immigrants and asylum-seekers housed in its parish.[10] A small group felt called to visit these people. Out of that visit they developed a course for those for whom English was not their first language. For many immigrants the members of this church were the only people in this new land whom they knew. They were also the only ones who had responded to them with welcome rather than suspicion and hostility.

An inner-city church found itself in a community that the local council had decided needed to be demolished. All the housing would come down in due course. The church recognized that their call was to stay with this community and serve it until no one was left. A number of church members who had been re-housed continued to come back to the church and community to strengthen that service until the last houses were vacated.

A rural church in seeking to discern its call recognized that it had many visitors to its church as the tower provided a wonderful view of the area and people were told about this by tourist information centres. In response the church built a visitors' centre in the grounds which was a meeting place, an exhibition centre and a cafe that served the needs of these visitors. The focus of those volunteers (over sixty of them from this one rural church) was in befriending those looking for someone to talk to. Many found solace and a listening ear as 'quality relationships' were established.

None of this comes easily or cheaply. It is costly to take time to stand back, pray and discern how God might be calling a church to respond to the divine vocation in their setting. It takes courage to wait until the sense of call has a clear shape, and courage to press on in the face of many obstacles and, often, plenty of objections. There is also the cost involved in sticking to such a vocation over the years, and, Nehemiah-like, not being distracted. There is also cost in 'doing one job and doing it well'. Yet the fruit of such persistence is almost always a rich harvest of grace in the local community, and in the church.

Second, in discovering people with a vision, passion and call to serve the local community. Ministry, as noted elsewhere, arises most fruitfully out of a sense of call from God. Church leaders need to be alive to where that vocation is happening. Not least do they need to do this as vision, passion and a sense of call alone can provide the motivation to keep going over the long haul, often when any fruits from their labours are pretty meagre.

A couple with a real concern for children and young people joined a church, but they were the only couple with children still living at home. A couple of other people agreed to join them in seeking to do something. It took eight years before there were over ten children and young people involved in the church. Now, thirteen years since they started, there are twenty-five or more. The original couple have handed over the work to others. It has been a long haul but the youth work is now seen as one of the strengths of that church.

A church, in reflecting on its strengths, identified its be-
reavement work as one of them. That was certainly the
impression church members had gained from their non-
churchgoing neighbours. But it had not always been so.
When they stopped to explore how that had come about,
those present identified four or five things that had caused
it to happen. They estimated that this work had become a
strength over a period of twelve to fifteen years.

How have these churches kept going over the long haul, even when initial
fruit was limited, or even lacking altogether? It was a sense of *vision,
passion* and *vocation*, in just a few, that was the source of the sustaining
energy over this long period.

Generosity in self-giving love

From the story of the church in Carthage, through the exhausting work
of the abolition of slavery, to the modern-day story with which the last
chapter closed, sacrificial service is one of the great distinguishing marks
of Christian service. It flows out of people being so touched by the
wonder and grace of God that they respond in kind, with overflowing
generosity vastly beyond the bounds of duty alone. We cannot create
such freely chosen service, but we can (through nurturing a healthy
church) create the circumstances in which such love can flourish and
find expression. Equally, seemingly small acts of kindness, like the
churchwarden shaking the hand of an elderly lady as told in the story
above, are acts of generosity that bear fruit out of all proportion to the
act itself. Sometimes love shows itself by the littleness of the things it is
willing to do.

Mission as the practice of an integrated spirituality

At the heart of the re-working of the church's engagement in mission and
evangelism we need to find a way in which spirituality, the coming of the
kingdom, integrity and self-giving love can come together. One valuable
aid to achieving that is through the use of what is called the 'pastoral
cycle', though it might better be described as the 'mission cycle'. It is a
simple framework for reflecting, from a theological rather than secular
perspective, on what we are doing in any mission venture. This 'mission
model' is equally valuable as an 'evangelism model'.

It comes originally from the Church in South Africa where it was
expressed in the three-stage process as *see–judge–act*. In the process

the *seeing* is about taking time to reflect on the situation we are engaged with and what action we discern as being needed. The *judging* is about reflecting theologically on what is going on, on where we see God at work in the situation and what we understand is God's call to us in that situation. The final stage of *acting* is when, in response to what we see, and how we judge that God is calling us, we take action. A worked example is to be found on pages 199–201 in the Resources section.

Conclusion

This book deliberately ends on the subject of mission, of the church engaging in God's purposes of love for all. The heart of the gospel is the wonder of God's love in Christ evidenced in his coming into our world in the context of poverty and in his dying at the hands of a brutal torturing regime. It is supremely not just proclaimed but *demonstrated*, when Christ's followers today reflect something of the richness and cost of that love in their own actions.

An early Christian letter (the epistle to Diognetus) sums up how the early Church was a living demonstration of God's costly love. If, by the grace of God, the Church today could recapture its clarity of 'what it's all about' and, as led by the Spirit, discern God's call on their lives, who knows but we too could be part of the rich tapestry of the 2,000-year story of the grace of God made evident in the lives of ordinary people with ordinary faith in an extra-ordinary God. It is essentially the story of a Church not afraid to live distinctive lives that reflect the character, ministry and mission of Christ himself.

> Christians are not distinguished from the rest of mankind by country, or by speech, or by dress. They do not dwell in cities of their own, or use a different language, or practise a peculiar life. This knowledge of theirs has not been proclaimed by the thought and effort of restless men; they are not champions of a human doctrine, as some men are. But while they dwell in Greek or barbarian cities according as each man's lot has been cast, and follow the customs of the land in clothing and food, and other matters of daily life, yet the condition of citizenship which they exhibit is wonderful, and admittedly strange. They live in countries of their own, but simply as sojourners; they share the life of citizens, they endure the lot of foreigners; every foreign land is to them a fatherland, and every father-land a foreign land. They marry like the rest of the world, they breed children, but they do not cast their offspring adrift. They have a common table, but yet not common. They exist in the

flesh, but they live not after the flesh. They spend their existence upon earth, but their citizenship is in heaven. They obey
the established laws, and in their own lives they surpass the
laws. They love all men, and are persecuted by all. They are
unknown, and they are condemned; they are put to death, and
they gain new life. They are poor, and make many rich; they
lack everything, and in everything they abound. They are dis-
honoured, and their dishonour becomes their glory; they are
reviled, and repay insult with honour. They do good, and are
punished as evildoers; and in the punishment they rejoice as
gaining new life therein … In a word, what the soul is in the
body, Christians are in the world.[11]

Here, certainly, is a Church that is living out of a sense of vocation, and
has not lost its nerve, in living by a distinctive perspective on life brought
to it through the life of Christ. God grant that such might be said of our
churches in the years to come.

For further help see *Part 3: Resources*, 'Introduction', pp. 137–9, 'Study questions',
pp. 177–9, and 'Leaders' resources', p. 181, pp. 197–8, pp. 199–201 and pp. 202–4.

Part 3:

Resources

Introduction

This material is designed for use by individuals, small groups, and leadership groups (such as staff teams, ministry teams and PCCs). It can also form the basis for sermon series, small group study guides and for quiet days. Suggestions of how this material might be used are set out below. Beyond these suggestions, creative adaptation to local needs is strongly encouraged. Fit the material to your situation.

Most individuals and groups are likely to want to pay particular attention to the *Foundations* section of the book (Part 1). They may then want to explore just one (certainly one at a time) of the subjects covered by the *Practicalities* section (Part 2). For groups this would make a natural five-session course. Leadership groups would benefit from taking the same approach, but may wish to focus in greater depth on one of the *Practicalities* issues. In doing so they would be well advised to identify a Christian distinctive on which the church's re-visiting of their chosen area of church life can be based.

Whether using this material for personal study, in a group, or among leaders, there is no need to work through it chapter by chapter. An individual or a group may simply want to pursue one issue, for example, 'What's it all about?', or 'Re-working giving'. Or, a number of chapters would work well as the basis for a PCC away day, giving opportunity to stand back from the 'tyranny of the urgent' to engage with the things that matter more.

The material will, hopefully, be the starting point for a deeper exploration than one session. Chapters built around a Christian distinctive will work best when explored over a sustained period. Using this material may lead to wanting to take things further than this book goes. Clergy can be a key resource here. They do not know everything, but their training should have helped them to find out where to find additional resources. If all else fails, try an internet search engine or Wikipedia!

The goal in all this is to discover more about our relationship with God and how it is to find expression in personal and corporate life. It is also important to keep in mind the aim, namely the *practice* of the knowledge of God. The goal is to change attitudes, priorities and actions so that what is done in the life of the church may aid personal and corporate living of the faith.

Session structure

Each session has four elements, as follows:

1   **Biblical exploration**: this roots the session in the riches of the Church's foundation documents (allow 15–20 minutes).

2   **Chapter exploration**: beginning with a five-minute review of the chapter by someone briefed beforehand to explain the basic argument of the chapter for those who have not read it. This explores the main issues raised in the chapter. (For timings see below.)

3   **In-depth exploration**: this looks in greater depth at one aspect of the subject. (For timings see below.)

4   **Spiritual exercise**: using the one from the chapter (if exploring Chapters 1–5), or repeating one of those (if exploring Chapters 6–10), or introducing one of your own (allow 15–20 minutes).

Assuming a 90-minute session, it is suggested that 15–20 minutes are allowed for the *Biblical exploration* and the *Spiritual exercise*. This will leave 50–60 minutes for the *Chapter exploration* and the *In-depth exploration*. It will work best to decide which element to focus on and so allocate more time to that.

It is important that, in managing the *Spiritual exercise*, this is done in an unhurried way, and not squeezed into the end of a full session. It might work well to do it between the *Chapter exploration* and the *In-depth exploration*. Equally, it would work well to start the session with it. It is best to be led by someone who has enough advanced notice for them to do the exercise themselves three or four times before the session so that they are familiar with it and can focus on helping others to do the same.

Good preparation always pays off. If the material is being worked at by a group, it is likely to be particularly effective if someone is planning ahead and inviting members of the group to contribute by preparing to read up and share some insights in a few sessions' time. For example, if the group is going to have a session on Chapter 3, 'Rich resources', it would be good to find out if anyone in the group has an interest in an aspect of church history, liturgy, the lives of the saints, or any spiritual tradition that they would like to prepare to share in that session. When doing this, the clearer the brief is, the better it is likely to work. This will include how long their whole 'slot' should be kept to, a suggested length and form of input, how long to let others explore the subject, and some possible 'discussion starters'. It is always good when doing this to follow the maxim: never overestimate people's information – or underestimate their intelligence!

Perhaps the most important thing to remember is that this material is intended to be highly flexible, so be creative and imaginative in planning and preparation. By all means start from the material given, but see it as a way in to a previously, relatively unexplored territory in which Robert Warren is not the only guide, and in which there may be hidden treasures of insight, experience and knowledge hidden away in the group itself. Use the material like clay in the potter's hands that can be shaped in a host of different ways; not as pottery out of the kiln whose use is fixed and unyielding.

Study questions

Chapter 1: *What's it all about?*

1 Biblical exploration

The 'Biblical roots' box (page 5) identifies a number of people whose encounter with God was foundational to all they had to offer. Invite two or three people beforehand to identify a key passage for each of these encounters and be ready to lead a five-minute reflection on their chosen passage.

Alternatively, work in triplets, focused on just one such character, identifying the key issues in their relationship with God. Each triplet could then share two or three insights from the study with the rest of the group, before the group decide what actions to take and then pray together.

2 Chapter exploration

The basic thesis of the book is set out in this chapter. It is that the purpose, and reason for the existence of the Church, is the pursuit of the knowledge of God.

Another way of putting it

Make a list of other ways in which you would wish to describe the purpose of the Church. *Do not discuss them at this stage*, simply list them until you have at least six alternatives. Then consider the various alternatives and come up with your own way of expressing what Church is all about.

An alien world

- *Either:* Imagine that a visitor from another world, whether African, Asian or Martian, spent this last week in your church. **What do you think they would conclude that church is all about?**

- *Or:* Choose one of the (shorter) epistles (Philippians, Colossians, 1 Peter, 1 John) and give people 5–10 minutes (preferably with paper and pencil) to cast their eyes over the text with the following questions in mind.

What do you think the members of this New Testament Church would make of what they found among us?

What would they be surprised to find, and what would they be surprised to find missing from church life today?

3 In-depth exploration

Mapping our experience of God

Working with the 'map' of how the knowledge of God is expressed in three modes or dimensions, consider:

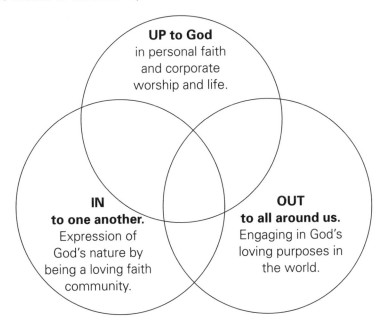

Explore any, or all, of these reflections on this 'map', and/or add your own questions.

■ *In terms of my own initial journey into faith, which dimension began the process and how did it take me into the other ones?*

■ *In terms of my journey of faith, since that initial stage, who, where or what has most inspired me with the living out of all three dimensions working together?*

■ *In which of these dimensions am I most/least aware of the presence of God, and which one seems to be the one that needs most attention at present?*

■ *In which of these dimensions is our church most/least clearly connecting with God, and where does it most need to focus?*

■ *How might we communicate that to the leadership/ membership? What steps could we take to play our part in the church's focus on that aspect of our relationship with God?*

Key books to aid further reflection and action

David Runcorn, *The Road to Growth Less Travelled,* Grove Books, 2008.

Robert Warren, *The Healthy Churches' Handbook,* CHP, 2004.

---

4 *Spiritual exercise*

See pages 13–14.

In the final issue

What actions do I/we plan to take to explore, and give expression to, the heart of Christian faith explored in this chapter?

Chapter 2: *Overcoming obstacles*

1 Biblical exploration

Turn to the 'Biblical roots' box (page 15) and explore any one (or more) of those and/or add your own further incidents and passages that speak more directly to you.

Consider what the response was in each situation and identify the implications for our living today and for our addressing obstacles in church and in all of life.

2 Chapter exploration

Summary of the obstacles to a practice of the knowledge of God

The chapter identifies the following:

The tyranny of the urgent: the pressure of the urgent and sheer busy-ness of modern life leaves us no time to stop and reflect on what we are doing, what really matters and what we do not currently have time for. As Bishop Laurie Green has put it:

> Many parish churches overwhelm themselves with actions, meetings and projects that are not necessarily directed by careful theological reflection, and may in fact be a squandering of their energies and resources rather than a faithful commitment to engage incarnationally with God in the world.[1]

When we get caught up in the tyranny of the urgent we can easily be more busy than effective. Daring to stop and having the courage to do so are vital to this end.

Blurred vision: This section identified a number of ways in which our thinking can become distorted and lacking a proper theological basis. These include:

- **Silo thinking**: causing the 'spiritual' to be kept in a separate compartment while most of church life is shaped by a secular, market culture.

- **Thinking organizationally rather than organically**: treating the church as an organization rather than as a living, dynamic community, limits our thinking.

- **Confusing 'means' and 'goals'**: too easily the usual means of dealing with an issue are treated as goals, when what we need to do is think clearly about the real, theological goal. Then we hold fast to that but think creatively and flexibly about a range of means. If some 'means' do not work, we should look for others, but not abandon the goal.

■ **Losing sight of God's agenda, gift and timing**: it is so easy to think that Church, and mission, are things we do for God rather than the divine means of incorporating us into God's plans and purposes. Looking for, waiting for, and working with the grace of God are at the heart of good leadership.

3 In-depth exploration

Framework for exploring and reflection on the obstacles we face

With these factors in mind, personally and/or as a group, we need to:

1 Discern what are the obstacles we face which are not covered in this chapter?

2 Discern what are the top three obstacles to growth in the knowledge of God and its outworking in my/our life?

3 Consider Mark 1 and look for obstacles Jesus experienced and what he did about them.

4 Spiritual exercise

See pages 24–5.

Key books to aid further reflection and action

Stephen Cottrell, *Do Nothing to Change your Life*, CHP, 2007.
It is a great resource to help shift our attitudes to and behaviour about busy-ness.

Laurie Green, *Let's Do Theology*, Mowbray, 1990, is a fine book on helping churches to think and act theologically.

In the final issue

What actions do I/we plan to take to overcome the obstacles to our personal and/or corporate living out the Christian faith?

Chapter 3: *Rich resources*

1 Biblical exploration

Select just one or two of the following areas to explore.

a Patriarchs building altars

Consider one, some, or all the following texts. In a group it could work well to get people in pairs to tackle any one of the incidents and come up with their answer to the question set out below.

- Genesis 8.20: Noah after the Flood.
- Genesis 12.1–8: Abraham responds to the call of God.
- Genesis 13.1–13: Abraham returns to his first altar to discern God's mind.
- Genesis 13.14–17: Abraham sets up a further altar to mark the place of blessing.
- Genesis 26.23–25: Isaac meets God and builds an altar.
- Genesis 33.18–20: Jacob builds an altar when he eventually makes it 'home'.

What do they have to say to us about how best to remember, with thanksgiving, life-changing moments in which God has shown us the way we are to choose? What might our 'altars' look like today?

b Festivals and liturgies: Deuteronomy 8

What do these festivals and their associated liturgies have to say to us today?

c Living in thanksgiving

Have available the list of thanksgiving texts set out in the box on page 99.

Here are two steps we can take to build the practice of thanksgiving (gratitude) to God and to others into our lives.

d *Part 1*: Giving thanks to God

Identify five things you want to give thanks for; look for a varied list. Probably after the session it would be good to make a longer list, elsewhere, first. Then start to do these things and let your experience guide you into selecting a balanced range in both lists. Make sure, in your first list, that God gets a mention at some point!

Take five minutes a day to say this list (out loud is best), adding any other thoughts that come to mind.

e *Part 2*: Giving thanks to others

This may be people, activities, occasions, etc., and include expressing appreciation and giving affirmation. Again, make a longer initial list, then get it down to just five. Once or twice a week, review this list and put a tick against anything that you have put into practice (and give thanks for that!).

2 Chapter exploration

It is good to explore the roots of our own spiritual heritage (most of us have roots in one of the main spiritual traditions of the Church). Discovering who the key people were and which are the key books and other resources that help us learn, and practice more, is a great aid to spiritual growth. Doing this in a group, rather than on our own, means that we can explore different elements of different traditions through which we can have a more whole picture of the resources the Church has built up over 2,000 years.

To consider

This chapter identifies several rich resources that sustain faith, namely:

- Scripture.
- Our spiritual heritage.
- Church history.
- Liturgy.
- Word and sacrament.
- People.
- Grace.
- Weakness.

What other resources, not included in that list, would you want to add?

Which of these have been of most significance in your spiritual journey?

Tell us how that has happened.

Is there an order of importance for the elements in this list, if so why, and how does this happen for you?

3 In-depth exploration

This is best done by inviting members of the group, a few weeks in advance of this session, to find out something about our heritage, including reading up about the stories of some of the saints who have been shining examples of our spiritual heritage.

They could then be asked to take five minutes to introduce what they have found. This could be followed by general discussion, led by someone other than the person introducing the heritage aspect, or saint. Probably three such inputs are suitable.

Consider ending this section with short prayers of thanksgiving for those who have gone before us.

4 Spiritual exercise

See pages 37–8.

Key books to aid further reflection and action

Richard Foster, *A Spiritual Formation Workbook*, HarperSanFrancisco, 1993.
Author of a number of books from the evangelical tradition, including *Celebration and Discipleship*, Hodder & Stoughton, 1980; *Freedom and Simplicity*, SPCK, 1981; and *Prayer*, Hodder & Stoughton, 2008, yet going beyond that, Richard Foster is a founder member of Renovare, a movement for spiritual renewal. In their key book, he (and fellow authors James Smith and Lynda Graybeal) explore the spiritual life of Jesus and six spiritual traditions; namely the *Contemplative*, *Holiness*, *Charismatic*, *Social Justice*, *Evangelical* and *Incarnational* traditions. These can either be explored as a whole course, or simply be used to tap into the key insights and resources of each of these traditions. This would be a good way of learning more about 'our' tradition as well as about other traditions that would enrich our faith. If the group wishes to pursue this line in more depth, this would make for a good six-session follow-up course.

David Runcorn's book, *Spirituality Workbook: A Guide for Explorers, Pilgrims and Seekers*, SPCK, 2006, opens with a section on insights from Christian History and Tradition in which he helpfully introduces five great traditions of Christian spirituality. This is a briefer introduction to the spiritual traditions than the Renovare Spiritual Formation Workbook.

Dennis Linn, *Sleeping with Bread: Holding what gives you life,* Paulist Press, 1994.
A wonderful and wonderfully accessible introduction to the Ignatian discipline of *Examen*. *Examen* is an examination of conscience and a way of review and reflection on the past (whether today, this week, month, year, decade or any time-frame). The book is only 72 pages long including a number of full-page drawings, so it does not take long to read: just a lifetime to practise. It gives the impression of being a children's book but it is very much for adult believers. A group could very usefully use this as the basis for doing regular *examen* exercises as part of their life.

Robert Warren's, *An Affair of the Heart,* Highland, 1994, includes prayer exercises at the end of each chapter designed to enlarge our practice of prayer and helping us to stretch our prayer muscles beyond their normal use. It is the basis for the five-session course, *Life Source,* designed for small groups.

Abbot Christopher Jamison, of Worth Abbey, has written books that accompany the television series on *The Monastery* and *Silence*. They include: *Finding Happiness* (Phoenix, 2009), *Finding Sanctuary* (Phoenix, 2007). These would be very helpful for individuals to read, pray and work through as well as for groups to explore.

Roberta Bondi, *To Pray and to Love: Conversations on Prayer with the Desert Fathers*, Burns & Oates, 1991.
Instructive integration of prayer and action from the perspective of the Desert Fathers. By linking prayer and action this book not only does justice to the monastic movement but re-connects spirituality with mission and service.

In the final issue

What actions do I/we, plan to take to draw upon more fully, and live in the light, of the rich heritage of faith in which we stand?

Chapter 4: *Living the Christian distinctives*

1 Biblical exploration

Read through the Sermon on the Mount (Matthew 5—7).

■   If doing so personally, read one section at a time/day.

■   If doing so in a group, encourage people to read it through before the group meets and come with their thoughts about the *distinctive things about the Christian way* that can be drawn from this teaching.

and/or

■   Reflect on one Gospel, scanning its pages, and make a note of any distinctive things about the 'way of Christ' that strike you.

2 Chapter exploration

a What is a 'distinctive'?

In the light of our reading of the chapter, or hearing the introduction of it, how would we describe to someone else what is meant by a Christian distinctive?

b Other important distinctives

There are a number of distinctives addressed in this chapter and elsewhere in the book. They are: *Listening, Vocation, Being, Spirituality, Generosity, Self-giving love, Community.*

What other things should be included on our church's list of the key distinctives that we should be exhibiting individually and as a church?

c Developing the distinctives

Consider the process outlined on page 150 for developing the distinctives, with a view to addressing the following questions:

What other steps do we consider need to be added to this list?

Which is the key distinctive for this group (or church) to develop, and where do we think we should be making a start?

The process outlined for developing any distinctive:

- Decide.
- Consult early.
- Look for diversity.
- Identify outcomes.
- Whole-system infection.
- Keeping going.

---

3 In-depth exploration

Developing our listening skills

Three listening quotations

Being heard is so close to being loved that for the average person, they are almost identical.
David Augsburger: *Caring Enough to Hear and be Heard* (Regal Books, 2009)

How could I have been so blind to what is *the* indispensable element to loving people – *listening*?
Peter Scazzero, *The Emotionally Healthy Church*, Zondervan, 2003.

Contrary to conventional wisdom, what most people need is a really good listening to. Anon.

A listening exercise

Form groups of three, but it is probably best not to have both members of a couple in the same group; however, as far as possible, let people choose where to go.

Duplicate the script in the box on page 151 and say that each person will have a turn at each of these three roles, operating as Sharer, Listener and Explorer. Each group should choose which order they go in.

The **Sharer** starts by sharing something appropriate that matters to them. People might be given a specific question to address, such as:

- something that is occupying my attention at present;
- what I feel about the state of the Church today;
- what concerns me about politics at present;
- the best moment for me in the last few months.

Or simply: *share your earliest/most formative/most recent experience of God.*

The Sharer shares – in five minutes – their response to the subject that has been identified. Encourage people to share not just what they *think* but what they *feel* about the subject. No interruptions, even if they get facts wrong.

Sharer: honestly, appropriately, out of our own experience.

Listener: entering into and drawing out the other person's experience of, and insights about, life: *rather than rushing to share ours.*

Explorer: issues raised and the light that faith throws on our experience. *Good conversations open up subjects and change the perspective of participants.*

After four minutes, groups are told 'One minute', then, after five minutes, 'Please finish off now.'

The **Listener** now takes over. Their task is, essentially, to *draw out the person* who has just been sharing. The Listener's role is not to talk about their response or their view, or to discuss what was said. Rather, their task is to discover and uncover more about what the Sharer thinks and feels and was trying to communicate. Obviously there will be conversation between the Sharer and the Listener. The Explorer can contribute too, but needs to hold back to allow the other two to do most of the talking.

Again, the 'one-minute' warning followed, at the five-minute mark, by 'Time's up now.'

The **Explorer** then leads the conversation, in which all three take part equally. The Explorer's task is to engage both the Sharer and Listener in a conversation about the *issues* raises. The idea here is to take the subject beyond the purely personal into the realm of reflecting on life and what matters to us. This conversation can go in many different directions. A good conversation involves people sharing something of themselves and gaining new insights about others and about life. Their thoughts and comments may help others, but that is not the goal. We are not here to sort each other out but to be real with each other.

Again, the 'one-minute' warning followed, at the five-minute mark, by 'Time's up now.'

Then the roles change round in the groups and another question is addressed.

If there is time for each one to *share, listen* and *explore*, that will take 45 minutes. Allowing an hour makes sense and gives time for the whole group to reflect together on the experience, including which role they found most difficult/enjoyable.[2]

When done in an ongoing group it is good to repeat the exercise two or three times a year and reflect on ways in which our listening and conversational skills are developing.

Key books to help prepare for action

Peter Scazzero, *The Emotionally Healthy Church: A strategy for discipleship that actually changes lives*, Zondervan, 2003.
The story of one church that addressed the distinctive of being *emotionally healthy*.

Mark Yaconelli, *Contemplative Youth Ministry*, SPCK, 2006.
Not just about youth work. The story of someone discovering how to help a church develop the distinctive of being a *contemplative* church. See further under Key Books at end of Chapter 5 below.

---

4 Spiritual exercise

See page 51.

In the final issue

What actions do I/we, plan to take to identify the distinctive way in which God is calling me/us to live the faith today?

Chapter 5: *Nurturing spirituality*

1 Biblical exploration

This material focuses on worship as a key factor in the nurturing of spirituality.

Consider the following three worship events from the perspective of:

- What we learn about the nature of God through this encounter.
- What we learn about the nature of worship and role of the worshipper.
- What we learn about the lifestyle that results from an encounter with God.

Isaiah 6.1–8 (13)	Isaiah encounters God in the Temple.
2 Corinthians 3.12–18	Paul describes the impact of encounter with God.
Revelation 4	The worship of heaven.[3]

Alternatively, give everyone a printed copy of Psalm 51.15–17, Isaiah 58.4–12 and Micah 6.8, and consider the implications for us of the intended fruits of worship.

2 Chapter exploration

The chapter highlighted the following areas and ways in which individual and corporate spirituality needs to be understood and nurtured, namely:

- *A defining moment*: what do we mean by spirituality?
- *The shape of Christian spirituality*: yielded, integrated, communal, transforming.
- *A fully engaged spirituality.*
- *Aspects of nurturing spirituality:* Worship, transcendence in worship, small groups, 'quiet days', the spiritual disciplines, ordinary church life, the relational dimensions.

Note: *worship* is dealt with more fully in the next sections (3) and (4), while *small groups* are dealt with more fully in Chapter 7 and the Resources for that chapter.

- *Quiet days*: and how they can help.
- *Spiritual disciplines*: as a key way to build prayer patterns into personal and corporate life.
- *Ordinary church life*: and how spirituality can be nurtured in it.
- *The relational dimension*: a crucial way in which spirituality is communicated.
- *In practice*: one church's story and what we can learn from it.

Identify the order of importance and relevance of the above elements and explore them in that order, or simply select one or two to consider.

The basic question is: *Which of these elements has best helped our spiritual life, and what could be done to further strengthen the prayer and spiritual life of this church?*

3 In-depth exploration

What is worship?

The material that follows can be used as the basis for personal reflection, meditation and action. It can also be used for group study to aid our understanding, practice and preparation for worship. If used in a group, preparation is needed beforehand to decide how to structure the discussion. It could also form the basis for a *sermon series* on the subject of worship.

Introduction

The regular acts of worship of the Church are, arguably, the single most important way in which the spiritual life of the Church is expressed and renewed week by week. Our problem is often over-familiarity. Leaders of worship can 'knock a service together' in half an hour or so yet can easily fail to put their heart into it. As for worshippers, our problem is often that 'we have been coming to church for so long we have forgotten why we are coming'. For both, the measure of a 'good service' can often become merely whether we liked what we did, rather than whether we met with and gave loving and wholehearted attention to God. The key is in preparation that honours the God whom we come to worship and the work that we are doing.

Three vital preliminaries

An important first step is to consider what we are doing in worship. The nearest social equivalent of worship is theatre or a concert. However, in both of those there are two groups of people: performers and spectators. In worship there are no spectators, everyone is a 'performer', or better, a participant. Liturgy means, literally, 'the work of the people' so it is something in which everyone is taking part. Yes, there are people 'up front' who give a lead, but the worship is done by the whole community.

Particularly in our informal culture, it is all too easy to turn what is intended to be a three-dimensional act of worship into a two-dimensional meeting where the focus is all on what the participants are doing.

But worship is about God: worshipping him for who he is and what he has done. Sometimes we have to admit that an act of worship seems to have paid little attention to God. Yes, God was frequently mentioned ('in passing', one might say) but little real attention was on the God whom we had come to worship.

Not least in these days of straitened finances, we could think that a vital part of worship is taking our collection (or arranging for it to be paid by standing order through the bank). And we would be right. But the real offering that God is looking for is the bringing, and putting into his care and control, of our hopes, our plans, our failures, our living. Giving ourselves, and our undivided attention, is the offering pleasing to God. In doing so we watch and listen to discern what God desires to do with what we have given.[4]

What is worship?

In addressing the subject of worship, the obvious starting point is to define what we are talking about. Yet many of us who regularly worship, or lead worship, rarely stop to think what we are doing. Moreover, worship is such a rich subject that no one definition can adequately cover the whole subject. Some of the definitions that give shape to what we are doing are as follows:

Worship is ... *engagement with the ultimate meaning of life*. This is evident particularly in 'rites of passage' where a deep instinct is expressed that our lives are set in a wider, deeper significance within all reality; even when an understanding of the nature of God and his revelation in Christ is, at best, limited. While it is tempting for regular worshippers to despise such acts as 'empty rituals' they have something to teach us, for in them 'unchurched' people have grasped and expressed something vital about the nature of worship. It is the activity in which we relate our lives to the deeper meaning and purpose of life. As someone has put it: worship is about relating microcosm (my world) to macrocosm (all that is). We regular worshippers can all too easily miss that point because of our over-familiarity with the routines of worship.

Worship is ... *the response of the creature to the creator*. To worship is to give attention to God as creator and redeemer. To do so provokes a response, or rather a multitude of responses: praise and adoration, wonder and worship, humility, confession and repentance, attention to what he has to say to us, openness to receive the gift of his presence, a desire to share our concerns and compassion for a broken world, and a hunger to discover and do his will. In a phrase, to worship is to give loving attention to God.

Worship is ... *giving and receiving of love with God*. Worship is the expression of a relationship with God, and relationships are expressed, and develop, through both giving and receiving love. In this unequal relationship of creator and creature, it is the divine love that has, and always does, take the initiative; yet such is God's love that he delights in our giving of love – even in trusting God enough to be honest in confession about where we fall short of his purposes. The heart of worship is openness, to receive by faith and give in devotion, honesty and availability to God's purposes in our lives and in his world. Our 'chief end is to glorify God and enjoy him for ever'.[5]

Worship is ... *a way of life*. Worship cannot be limited to public acts of worship in a one- or two-hour event each week.[6] It is an approach to life. If worship 'in church' is to have any integrity it has to be lived out and made part of all we do. We cannot, in any authentic way, pay loving attention to God 'in church' and then spend the rest of the week 'doing our own thing'. So corporate worship, personal devotions, practising the presence of God, engaging with God's purposes in all of our living, are all part of a life of worship. For many of the prophets the real worship of God is the doing of justice.[7] As Bishop Michael Marshall is fond of saying at the end of an act of worship, 'The worship is over, let the service begin.'

In short, worship is encounter and engagement with, and response to, God.

Questions to ask throughout this exploration

What does this have to say about how we should prepare for worship?

What steps could we, individually, as a group, and as church, take to be better at giving ourselves to God in worship?

4 Spiritual exercise

See pages 69–70.

Alternatively, here (or in another session) consider using the following.

Five steps into the presence of God

Be still

Find as quiet and undisturbed a time and place as possible. Sit comfortably but upright. Begin by paying attention to your breathing, breathing out tensions and distraction, letting your body and mind relax.

Give yourself

Bring yourself, and the things that matter most to you and occupy your mind at present. Do not 'pray' about them, simply offer them to God, entrusting them to his care. Don't forget your joys and longings.

Give thanks

Give God thanks for what we 'take for granted':

- Our health and material comfort.
- The beauty of the world around us.
- Family and friends and all whom we love.
- Human creativity, music, art and society.
- God's love in Christ: mercy, guidance, protection.

Don't rush through a long list; better by far to linger, with gratitude, over just one or two of God's great gifts.

Give worship

Worship is about focusing on God. It is not about *getting God's attention* but about *giving our attention* to God. We can do this in a variety of ways, such as:

- in your own **words**: 'Praise you Lord for your love, your ...';
- in **God's names**: Rock, Shepherd, Saviour, Holy, Creator ...;
- a **scripture**: 'Our Father in heaven, hallowed be your name ...' *or:* a Psalm (e.g. 8, 19, 96, 100), the five hymns of heaven (Revelation 4, 5);
- with a **hymn**: 'O worship the Lord in the beauty of holiness ...';
- with **music**: play/sing something that aids worship of God;
- with **visuals**: using an icon or physical symbol of worship;
- with **touch**: holding/feeling a cross or other symbol;
- in **silence**: give wordless, loving attention to God;

Receive God's presence

In worship we become aware of God's presence. Now God's gift is to be present with us in all of life. We receive that gift as we yield ourselves to be part of God's loving purposes in the world, and as we let God express his nature in who we are and how we respond to life.

> Eternal God and Father,
> you create us by your power
> and redeem us by your love:

guide and strengthen us by your Spirit,
that we may give ourselves in love and service
to one another and to you;
through Jesus Christ our Lord. Amen

Key books to aid further reflection and action

Mark Yaconelli, *Contemplative Youth Ministry*, SPCK, 2006.
Remarkable story of one person's journey from activism to
contemplation in leadership and the development of a church culture.
This treats *contemplation* as a 'distinctive' within the terms of this
book.

David Runcorn, *Spirituality Workbook: A Guide for Explorers, Pilgrims
and Seekers*, SPCK, 2006.
Helpful 'primer' for the exploration and development of spirituality in
the life of the church. Includes summary of the main spiritual traditions
(pp. 9–50). Good to read and apply in connection also with the next
chapter on pastoral care.

Background reading

Richard F. Lovelace, *Dynamics of Spiritual Life: An Evangelical
Theology of Renewal*, Paternoster Press, 1970.
Fascinating, thorough and instructive history of healthy evangelical
spirituality (USA) in the last 300 years.

On worship

Richard Giles, *Creating Uncommon Worship: Transforming the Liturgy
of the Eucharist*, Canterbury Press, 2004.

Duncan Forrester, Ian McDonald and Gian Tellini, *Encounter with
God: An Introduction to Christian Worship and Practice*, T & T Clark
International, 2004.

Marva J. Dawn, *Reaching Out without Dumbing Down: A Theology of
Worship for This Urgent Time*, Eerdmans, 1995.

In the final issue

What steps can we take to enrich our, and others', encounters with
God in corporate and personal prayer times?

Chapter 6: *Re-working pastoral care*

1 Biblical exploration

Consider any of the following expressions of pastoral care:

Job
Why did Job's comforters get it so wrong?
(There will need to pre-reading and preparation to achieve this.)

Luke 24.13–35
Jesus on the road to Emmaus.
What can we learn from how Jesus handled this situation?

Galatians 6.1–10
Paul's encouragement to mutual pastoral care.
How can this be developed as a mark of our church life?

Alternatively, The 'one another' verses from the section entitled *The elements of pastoral culture*, on page 72 would provide a fruitful basis for considering the question: **What does it mean to pay loving attention to one another?**

Note: This biblical material is repeated in the Resources for Chapter 7: *Re-working home groups* (page 163). Those doing both studies need to use one of the alternatives here and one in conjunction with Chapter 7.

2 Chapter exploration

The chapter began with a definition of pastoral care as 'companionship into wholeness', with an understanding of mutuality in building up each other 'in the Lord' as the basis for an understanding that pastoral care is for all, not just those in 'need'.

The chapter itself would form a good starting point for discussion of a church's pastoral work, not least when it might be under review. Groups or individuals would be well advised to decide beforehand whether developing a *pastoral culture* or developing *pastoral care* was going to be their primary focus.

There are two sections to the chapter.

Part 1: Developing a pastoral culture looks at issues of mutual pastoral care (see pages 72–6):

■   Elements of a pastoral culture.

- ■   The style: mutual care.
- ■   The means: changing church culture.

A group or individual studying this material would benefit from addressing the question:

What does this say about my/our experience and my/our practice of mutual pastoral care in this church?

Part 2: Developing pastoral care looks at issues concerning the development of pastoral care work within the life of a church (see pages 76–82). See the Leaders' Resources section (pages 187–9) for more material.

3 In-depth exploration

The following material suggests some principles in mutual pastoral care and knowing how to respond to our own situations and those faced by others.

Living the gospel in all of life

The material that follows can be used as the basis for personal reflection, meditation and action. It can also be used for group study. If used in a group, preparation is needed beforehand to decide how to structure discussion of this material. It could also form the basis for a *sermon series*.

Notes:

1   This material is best handled in a way that does not restrict its application to relationships with church members only. Help the group to see its application to wider family and friends' circles and to work colleagues too.

2   This material would also work well in the '*In-depth*' section of Chapter 9 to explore how the way in which we live and handle ourselves and our lives can equip us to help others on the journey to faith.

To understand pastoral care as paying loving attention to others and being *companions into wholeness* is to recognize its missionary dimension. To handle our own lives as outlined in this chapter, will shape the way we relate to others in the whole of life. Indeed, giving and receiving such loving attention is one of the best ways of equipping us to 'be Christ for others'. In particular we can do this as we cultivate in our lives and in the life of our churches ...

- *The capacity to listen* and the willingness to give time to doing so. A number of research projects in recent years have sought to get in touch with people's experience of the spiritual and supernatural dimensions of life. All of the researchers report that the 'problem' they found was that simply asking people to share their experiences awakened in them a new desire to pursue the matter further. That left the researchers, who had set up the interviews on the basis of objective research, wanting to share their own faith and help others to explore faith in Christ, yet feeling constrained not to do so by the terms of their 'contract' with such people. It points, however, to a vital way in which faith might be awakened in others – just by listening and letting them tell their stories of encounters with God, the spiritual dimension of life and with the Church.[8]

- *The capacity to know yourself*, which is a fruit of giving and receiving pastoral care, is fundamental to helping others to come to terms with themselves. Moreover, the specifically Christian dynamics of repentance and forgiveness, experienced on a daily basis, are wonderful equipment for helping others to come to terms with their struggles.

- *The capacity to explore* an issue rather than jump straight into solution mode. When someone shares a concern with us, we all too easily want simply to 'tell them what the answer is' and what to do. What they are looking for is someone with whom they can look at the matter with fresh eyes. As the poet Kathleen Raine has put it: 'Beauty is the real aspect of things when seen aright and with the eyes of love.'

- *The willingness to give*. This is 'the whole law'. It is not primarily about giving money (though that is involved) but about giving hospitality to the marginalized, forgiveness to the 'enemy', truth to the tyrants and goodness to all. *Dispensing God's grace is the Christian's main contribution.*[9]

- *The courage to address conflict* and function in the role of a peacemaker. 'Overcoming evil with good' is one of the distinctives of the Christian faith. Few of us like to be involved in situations of conflict but it is often part of our calling.

- *The willingness to name the Name* and acknowledge Christ as the source of any contribution we make to individuals and communities as *companions into wholeness*.

How can we live this sort of life and help each other to live our faith like this?

4 Spiritual exercise

See Introduction to Resources: use one of the exercises from the end of Chapters 1–5, or introduce another appropriate exercise from your own experience.

Key books to aid further reflection and action

Alastair V. Campbell, *Rediscovering Pastoral Care*, Darton, Longman and Todd, 1986.
A most helpful re-working of pastoral care for a post-hierarchical culture.

Alan Jamieson, *A Churchless Faith: Faith Journeys Beyond The Churches*, SPCK, 2002.
Addressing the issues of the spiritual journeys by those moving 'beyond' the churches. Important for church leaders to understand what is going on in faith journeys as it affects existing members as well as, potentially, returning members.

James W. Fowler, *Faith Development and Pastoral Care*, Fortress Press, 1987.
Links together the previous two books and has a striking understanding of pastoral care that connects with mission, summed up in his definition of pastoral care as 'forming lives within the church for the purposes of Christian vocation in the world'.

In the final issue

What actions can we do to take forward, personally and corporately, the insights about pastoral care outlined in this chapter?

Chapter 7: *Re-working home groups*

1 Biblical exploration

Consider any of the following expressions of pastoral care:

Job   **Why did Job's comforters get it so wrong?**
(There will need to pre-reading and preparation to achieve this.)

Luke 24.13–35   Jesus on the road to Emmaus.
What can we learn from how Jesus handled this situation?

Galatians 6.1–10   Paul's encouragement to mutual pastoral care.
How can this be developed as a mark of our church life?

Alternatively, the 'one another' verses from the section entitled *The elements of pastoral culture*, on page 72 (last line of first paragraph of the section) would provide a fruitful basis for considering the question: **What does it mean to pay loving attention to one another?**

A further alternative: those planning to do the 'small group vocation exercise' might prefer to move straight to the two passages at the start of that material, namely: Isaiah 42.1–4 and Matthew 9.35–37, to be found on page 164.

2 Chapter exploration

Here are some questions that a group, individual or leadership might want to use to help them engage with the material presented in this chapter.

Owning and addressing the issues (pp. 83–85):

How far do we go along with this diagnosis, what would we want to add or change to it, and what are the practical implications for us?

Strategies to renew the role of home groups

- Recognize the bigger picture (p. 85).
- Affirm the community basis of church life (p. 88).
- Recover the goal of home groups (p. 88).
- Re-connect with spirituality (p. 89).
- Turn the whole church outwards (p. 90).

■ Resource the leaders (p. 90).
■ Develop alternative models (p. 92).

How far do we go along with this diagnosis, what would we want to add or change to it, and what are the practical implications for us?

3 In-depth exploration

The following exercise is designed to help small groups consider the task that they share in.

Small group vocation exercise[10]

The God revealed in scripture is a God who acts, especially on behalf of the poor and those in need. This is very evident in the Old Testament prophets and especially so in the ministry of Jesus. Consider what these two passages say about God's care for others and our part in that compassion:

> Here is my servant, whom I uphold,
> my chosen, in whom my soul delights;
> I have put my spirit upon him;
>   he will bring forth justice to the nations.
> He will not cry or lift up his voice,
>   or make it heard in the street;
> a bruised reed he will not break,
>   and a dimly burning wick he will not quench;
>   he will faithfully bring forth justice.
> He will not grow faint or be crushed
>   until he has established justice in the earth;
>   and the coastlands wait for his teaching. (Isaiah 42.1–4)

> Then Jesus went about all the cities and villages, teaching in their synagogues, and proclaiming the good news of the king-dom, and curing every disease and every sickness. When he saw the crowds, he had compassion on them, because they were harassed and helpless, like sheep without a shepherd. Then he said to his disciples, 'The harvest is plentiful, but the labourers are few; therefore ask the Lord of the harvest to send out labourers into his harvest.' (Matthew 9.35–37)

Consider

■ In what ways was Jesus fulfilling the Old Testament prophecy?
■ How does God want us to be part of this work today?

Share

Where we see this at work today and in the history of the Church.

It would be good to get anyone, willing to do so, to do some research about:

- early Church and monastic service of the poor;
- St Francis of Assisi;
- the impact of Methodism/Evangelicals on social reformation in the nineteenth century;
- any other actions and individuals that people would like to highlight.

Invite them to share (within an agreed time-frame) what they have discovered.

How shall we serve?

A pond goes stagnant if water is coming in but there is no way for it to get out. The same is true for groups, as someone has said, 'No group can be healthy unless it has a task beyond itself to fulfil.' So what is our task, mission, calling?

Consider some of these options and what they have to say to us.

- *Supporting one another to live out our faith in the whole of life:* This may well be the right focus for a good number of groups. However, we need to go beyond vague hopes and good intentions. That is best done by identifying what specific steps we will take to do so. Also, what outcomes (say, in one year's time) should we look for and work for, as evidence that this is happening?

- *Church life:* It may well be that the group relates to some particular aspect of church life. How can we express this focus in terms of specific steps we commit ourselves to take and specific outcomes we are going to work for?

- *Prayer support:* It might be that someone in the group has a key role (e.g. as foster parents, or a head teacher, local councillor, etc.) whose work and area of service we want to support actively, with a particular focus on prayer (but not limited to that). That will involve us identifying something specific, measurable, we can take as a group.

- *Community needs:* Are there needs in the community in which some of us are already engaged and others would want to support us actively in? Or is there an issue we want, as a group, to engage with? If so, we need to identify what steps we need to take to make, sustain and measure that engagement.

- *Wider justice issues:* Is there a wider issue in our country (e.g. homelessness, drugs, poverty, drugs, pollution, etc.) that is a natural focus for us as a group? If so, again, specific plans need to be developed in order for this to become something that we can sustain, and measure, over the long term.

- *World mission:* This might cover support for missionaries and/or missionary societies and focuses, or global issues such as climate change, overcoming poverty, sickness, conflict, etc. Once more, we need to translate an interest in something into a specific and sustained programme of measureable actions.

- *Some other focus* not covered by any of the above.

Accountability

There is much to be said for making the group accountable to someone outside the group for the mission focus. Obviously it would be good to keep the leadership of the church informed of what it is. Indeed, it would be good to invite them to respond to our plans and help develop them further. Moreover, it is good to have someone to whom we give permission to come to the group (say two or three times a year) and find out how things are going and to help us address any issues and obstacles we are meeting along the way.

Health warning!

It is important to remember that we are looking for a *single* focus, so what follows are possible options, not a list of things we ought to take on. That would crush the group. The goal, rather, is to discern how God might be calling us to give an outward-looking focus to the group. It may take several meetings, prayer and talking together before we come to a consensus that seems like the task God is calling us to. Better to get the right focus after months, than to snatch at 'any old answer' in one session.

4 Spiritual exercise

See Introduction to Resources: use one of the exercises from the end of Chapters 1–5, or the alternative for the previous session, or introduce another appropriate exercise from your own experience.

Key books to aid further reflection and action

Joseph R. Myers: *The Search to Belong: Rethinking Intimacy, Community and Small Groups*, Zondervan, 2003.
An important new understanding of how people relate on four different levels: the public, social, personal and intimate. The implications of this for small groups and the life of the Church are then thoroughly investigated.

Emmaus: *Growth Book IV: Your Kingdom Come*, CHP.
The whole book is on mission, but of particular interest are pages 72–78, the Action Focus Session.

Leading an Emmaus Group, CHP, 1998.
… and not just an Emmaus Group. There is much in this little book of value for anyone seeking to lead any sort of small group.

In the final issue

What actions do I/we plan to take to aid the re-working of the relational dynamic in our church?

Chapter 8: *Re-working giving*

1 Biblical exploration

Here are three striking and highly instructive passages about the nature and dynamics of Christian giving. Exploration of any one of these passages is likely to be all that a group could do as part of one session, though returning to the other ones later would be a valuable additional exercise. Larger groups (e.g. PCCs) would benefit from forming three groups, each studying one passage, and reporting back to the whole group the key points from their study of the passages at the end of that study time.

1 Chronicles 29.1–22: David takes the lead in giving for the building of the Temple motivated by thanksgiving expressed in worship and joy.

Matthew 6.25–34: Jesus' teaching about generosity in the face of anxiety.

2 Corinthians 8.1–15: Paul's encouragement to generosity in response to grace.

In Chapter 8, in the section entitled 'The marks of Christian giving', the following distinguishing marks of Christian giving were noted (pp. 101–4):

- Relational – a response to love.
- Generous.
- Freely given.
- Self-giving.
- A priestly ministry.

In looking at any of the above passages it would be good to consider:

Which of these marks is most evident?

What other marks are evident besides those listed above?

How would the group want to sum up the distinctive marks of Christian giving?

Note: Groups that have not done the thanksgiving study and exercise from Chapter 3 might wish to substitute that for this Bible study.

2 Chapter exploration

The introduction and sections on 'The generosity distinctive' and 'Celebrating God's generosity' base the whole consideration in God's goodness and liberality.

Where have we encountered God's generosity, in creation, in the saints, in others who have touched our lives?

What lessons can we draw from these evidences of grace?

The thanksgiving study and exercise. See Chapter 3 and the note above, at the foot of the Bible exploration material.

The two sections on the motivation for and marks of Christian giving can be considered by addressing the following questions:

Where have we seen, in church history, in the lives of others, in our own experience, this sort of motivation and these sort of marks for giving and generosity (not just of money)?

How can we move into this sort of living and giving?

3 In-depth exploration

The website http://www.parishresources/givingforlife is commended for its five downloads, each one consisting of a Bible study, a life application and prayer response element. The five studies are entitled:

- Everything comes from God.
- Be active in your stewardship.
- Live within your means.
- Build up treasure in heaven.
- Give generously.

Simply choose the one (or more) sessions of most relevance to you/your group/church. Replace the Bible exploration above with the Bible material in the download.

4 Spiritual exercise

See Introduction to Resources: use one of the exercises from the end of Chapters 1–5, or the alternative for the previous session, or introduce another appropriate exercise from your own experience.

Key books to aid further reflection and action

Philip Yancy, *What's So Amazing About Grace?*, Zondervan, 1997.
Very fine book about the generosity in the heart of God, and its
outworking in the life of the believer. Essential reading for churches
seeking to explore and express God's generosity in the whole of its
life.

John Preston, *The Money Revolution: Applying Christian Principles to
Handling Your Money*, Authentic, 2007.
A great resource which does a fine job of integrating the spiritual
relationship with God to the way we see, handle and give our money.
Use in conjunction with the download material from http://www.
parishresources/givingforlife and its five sessions of material as
outlined above.

In the final issue

What actions do I/we plan to take to enable a more widespread
practice of generosity, including (but going well beyond) financial
giving?

Chapter 9: *Re-working evangelism*

1 Biblical exploration

A masterclass in helping others on the road to faith (Luke 24.13–25)

The road to (and from) Emmaus has much to teach us about helping others on the journey to faith. For Jesus it involved the following steps (read the passage first).

Listening

Where are you coming from? What is your starting point?

'What are you discussing together as you walk along?'

Our first task is to understand 'where people are at' and where they are coming from. What are their hopes and fears and concerns? In the short term it may take us in the opposite direction (towards Emmaus) from the one we want to get to (Jerusalem) but 'sitting where they sit' is a vital biblical principle and necessary first step.

Vulnerability

How do you feel? What has been your experience?

'We had hoped that he was the one.'

It is when we are real, honest and open with ourselves and with others that we are also open to God, grace and change. Discovering someone's past experience (including disappointments) about faith, the Church and God, is vital. So …

- Set an example – be real yourself.
- Create a climate of openness and honesty: no emotion is wrong, it is what we do with the emotions that makes for moral judgement.
- Affirm and protect those who make themselves vulnerable.

New insights

How about …? Have you thought of …?

'Were not our hearts burning within us while he talked?'

When we are real and honest, we are open to seeing things differently. That is the point at which new insights come. So …

- Be open to those moments of new insights.
- This is the moment when we can share our own experiences (but briefly!).
- Create an openness to new insights – welcome the awkward insights.
- Spot anyone having an 'Aha!' moment: affirm and protect the moment and them.

Learning experiences

Why not do/try ...?

'He took bread, gave thanks ... then their eyes were opened and they recognized him.'

All of us learn most by doing, by experiencing something that makes us see life differently. Hence the value of introducing people into any situation where they are likely to experience the presence and reality of God. This may be an act of worship, a group of believers/enquirers/or other situation.

- Resist the need to put people 'right' all the time.
- Enjoy the questions and searching together as a vital part of the journey.
- Expect to learn yourself.

Empowering

You can do it! Why not pray yourself?

'They got up and returned at once to Jerusalem.'

Encourage people to act upon their new-found faith:

- Affirm (more than tell) people when they suggest ideas and practical action.
- Give permission (rather than withhold permission) wherever possible.
- Trust people: work by the dictum 'You can do it', rather than 'Leave it to me'.

Critical mass

How about asking/including?

'There they found the Eleven, then the two told what had happened.'

It greatly helps people new to faith to meet with others who share that faith. We all need a critical mass of support to venture out on the journey of faith. Create situations where the newcomer to faith can feel part of a bigger group of believers.

■ Pay attention to strength/quality of conviction/commitment.
■ Find ways to affirm, nourish and develop conviction, vocation, commitment.

Vocation

What do you think God might want here?

'You are witnesses of these things, I am going to send you ...'

Expect those new to faith to sense God calling them to act on their faith. Be quick to spot tentative responses to God and be alongside people as they decide how to act.

■ Affirm and support newcomers to the faith as they step out in service and witness

Keep the faith focus

What do you want to do? Have energy for?

'Then they worshipped him and returned to Jerusalem with great joy.'

Protect people from being sucked into any religious over-activity. Help them keep the focus on 'what it's all about', namely knowing and worshipping God. So,

■ Help the new to faith to relax, enjoy God and deepen their sense of being.
■ Help them to begin a lifetime of loving and seeking after God.

What strikes us most about this story and process?

How does this ring true in our experience of coming to faith and helping others on the journey to faith?

What would we, from our own experience, want to add?

2 Chapter exploration

Defining our terms

The chapter begins with consideration of various terms that relate to evangelism.

What is new to us in these definitions?

What strikes us most in these definitions?

What are the practical implications of seeing things this way?

'Trends in evangelism': the chapter looks at the shifts from:

- event to process;
- gifted individual to priestly communion.
- doctrine to spirituality;
- speaking to listening;

Where, looking back, can we see these trends at work today?

What other trends have we noticed and what are the implications for us?

'The accompanied journey', 'The reality of the situation' and 'The greater reality' sections:

What is our response to the material in these three sections, and what are the practical implications?

3 In-depth exploration

a Articulating our faith

One of the most effective ways of learning to share our faith is by articulating our faith experience first to one another. Here are some questions that can help in that process.

Who, or what, most influenced my journey to faith?

From first interest to acknowledging Christ as Lord, how long did that journey take; and what were some of the key milestones on the way?

In what ways have I been aware of the presence of God in my life in recent times (weeks, months)?

What attitudes or actions I now practise arise out of my faith in God?

This work can be further developed by drawing on any, or all, of the 'Articulating the Faith' resources identified in the reading list in the box below.

b Articulating *their* faith

It has been argued in this book that one of the distinctives of the Christian faith is listening; and that this is so because the God of love calls us to pay loving attention to all. So in engaging with those who do not 'name the name of Christ', it may well be that our primary calling is to listen, and help others to reflect upon, their own experience.

Mark Yaconelli[11] helpfully suggests that this can be seen as a three-stage process of:

- *Noticing:* others' experience of the spiritual dimension of life, and helping others to notice their experience too.

- *Naming:* helping others to put a name, to enrich their understanding of that experience, and then to

- *Nurture:* the awareness of God that is emerging in their experience.

Look at the story of Janice Turner (pages 116–17) and imagine a friend had told you that story, what steps could you imagine taking to help her on that noticing–naming–nurturing process?

Or, if anyone in the group is in touch with someone who has shared a similar story, work with that person (or persons) to explore the steps they could take.

In doing this, remember the example of Jesus on the road to and from Emmaus, but use it as a springboard to other ideas, not a 'system' to slavishly follow.

4 Spiritual exercise

See Introduction to Resources: use one of the exercises from the end of Chapters 1–5, or the alternative for the previous session, or introduce another appropriate exercise from your own experience.

Key books to aid further reflection and action

Thorough Initiation

Peter Ball, *Adult Believing*, Mowbray, 1986.

John Finney, *Finding Faith Today*, Bible Society, 1996.

William Abraham, *The Logic of Evangelism*, William B. Eerdman, 1996.

Articulating the Faith

Janice Price, *Telling Our Faith Story*, Board of Mission, 1999.
A helpful introduction to talking with other believers about our faith.

James Lawrence: *Lost For Words: For All Who Think Evangelism is Not for Them*, CPAS, 1999.
Much used Course.

Dennis Linn's, *Sleeping with Bread: Holding what gives you life*, Paulist Press, 1994.
A wonderful and wonderfully accessible introduction to the Ignatian discipline of *Examen*. Great way to learn to articulate our faith.

Chapter 10: *Re-working mission*

1 Biblical exploration

Consider the implications for our view of mission of these passages:

Genesis 12.1–3: Abraham to be a blessing to all the families of the earth.

Isaiah 42.1–9: Israel to be a light to the Gentiles.

Matthew 25.31–46: Mercy and compassion for all as the hallmark of disciples.

What is God saying to us and call us to through these scriptures?

2 Chapter exploration

Looking at the terms that appear on page 121:
Where are we strongest/weakest in the areas identified here?

Considering 'The bigger picture' section (p. 122):
What does this have to say to us personally and corporately?

Consider the 'Mission as living the Christian distinctives' section (pp. 127–31).
Where might God be calling us to put the focus of our living at present?

3 In-depth exploration

Mission as expressing 'what it's all about'

This material seeks to connect the beginning of the book with its ending and all points in between. A good review and overview for those who have worked through the rest of the material.

Mission is essentially about what God is doing in his world to express his loving care for all creation and humanity. That care is focused on bringing people and situations into wholeness, including the wholeness of knowing God. God is at work in his world bringing all to the fulfilment of their nature and destiny: this is the kingdom of God, the places where God's purposes are coming into being. The Church does not have any mission itself: it is simply called to join in with God's mission. 'To participate in mission is to participate in the movement of God's love towards people, since God is a fountain of sending love.'[12]

All engagement in mission needs to begin with the exercise of spiritual discernment about what part God is calling us, the Church and each one of us individually, to play in those purposes of love. Prayer is not just the starting point; it is also the means by which our part is best conducted. Spirituality is part of the distinctive dynamic of all Christian service through which God, others and ourselves are brought together. In mission, perhaps above all, the upward relationship to God, the inward movement to others within the church as partners, and the outward movement to the world around come together as one whole. Again, David Bosch puts it: 'Mission is…the good news of God's love, incarnated in the witness of a community, for the sake of the world.'[13]

Because mission is part of the outworking of God's purposes, though it may often take us into meeting pressing physical needs, it will always take us beyond that. It will take us into costly yet life-giving relationships with God, to discover and do his will, and equally into costly yet life-giving relationships with others. Not least is this so because mission is an expression of the generosity of God to his world. Our calling is to see others in all their attractiveness to God and in their relationship to his loving purposes for them and for all creation. But it is also to share in their sufferings and struggles: 'A Christian is someone who shares the sufferings of God in the world.'[14]

Mission is essentially, therefore, a priestly ministry in which, through loving service, God and people are brought into living relationship. A key dynamic in this is that of *vocation*: discovering God's vision for the service of others and our part in it. As such it involves living out our knowledge of God, discerning his call, his ways, his surprises, his active grace and his call to self-giving and often sacrificial service. This vocation applies equally to individuals and to church communities; however, once we take vocation seriously and integrate it with every-member pastoral care, we soon discover the 'being and living' elements of the wider picture in the above framework, and the close relationship between spirituality and vocation. This, at its heart, is the living out of 'what it's all about', namely giving expression to the knowledge of God in the reality of daily living.

So what – in our own words – is mission all about?

Where and in what ways are we as a church engaging in mission?

What new insights have we gained about how mission works?

What do we now want to do about engaging in mission?

4 Spiritual exercise

See Introduction to Resources: use one of the exercises from the end of Chapters 1–5, or the alternative for the previous session, or introduce another appropriate exercise from your own experience.

Key books to aid further reflection and action

Laurie Green, *Let's Do Theology*, Mowbray, 1990, and Continuum, 2009: completely revised and updated version. A pastoral cycle resource book.

Ann Morisy, *Journeying Out: A New Approach to Christian Mission*, Morehouse, 2004.

Mark Yaconelli, *Contemplative Youth Ministry: Practising the presence of Jesus with young people*, SPCK, 2006.

Philip Yancy, *What's So Amazing About Grace?*, Zondervan, 1997.

In the author's view these are the best four books on mission practice. If a church were to give sustained attention to the implementing of these books there is little doubt that its effectiveness in mission would be greatly enriched. But it will take two or three years or more to do that. Do not dismiss Yaconelli's book because of the 'youth' focus. It can be read simply as contemplative ministry and is relevant to all of church life.

For *rural* churches, start with:

Alan Smith, *God-Shaped Mission*, Canterbury Press, 2008.

Andrew Bowden, *Ministry in the Countryside*, Continuum, 2003.

Leaders' resources

The materials in this section are designed for use particularly by those involved in churches in leadership and decision-making about the issues explored. They relate to the relevant chapters in the following ways.

Chapter 5: 'Nurturing spirituality'

'Leading worship' (1) and 'Preaching is ...' (2) are follow-ons from the In-depth exploration about worship. Although developed for work with those involved in these two ministries there is much value in working through these two documents with leaders and worshippers so that both can understand better the role of the other. So PCCs are a good place in which to explore these matters, as are choirs, worship groups and home groups where a leader in worship and/or preacher is present.

Chapter 6: 'Re-working pastoral care'

In seeking to develop pastoral care in a church, considering the second half of the chapter which covers:

- Growing pastoral care as the method.
- Identifying pastoral gifts.
- Growing a pastoral team.
- Deploying a listening team.
- Enjoying the fruits of an effective pastoral team.

And the question: ***How might these insights be applied in this situation?***

'Pastoral care principles' (3) is designed to be used by those involved in any way in a church's pastoral care work, or in any overall leadership in a church, including home group leaders. However, again, there is great value if such leaders explore these issues with those 'on the receiving end' of such ministries so that a fuller picture and a culture of mutual learning can be developed.

Chapter 7: 'Re-working home groups'

Strategies to renew the role of home groups (pp. 85–92), looking at the following sections of the chapter:

- Recognize the bigger picture.
- Affirm the community basis of church life.
- Recover the goal of home groups.
- Re-connect with spirituality.
- Turn the whole church outwards.
- Resourcing the leaders.
- Develop alternative models.

Either consider the order of priorities in your situation for each of these sub-sections and address them in their order of importance, or go though them one at a time; or address this basic question, after each section or once at the end of the discussion:

What are the relevant issues raised for us here, and what should our response be?

Chapter 8: 'Re-working giving'

'Structures for Christian giving' (4): unless specifically requested by the leadership of the church, it is probably not appropriate to spend much time on these details. However, it would be good to give some consideration to the suggested plan and, if thought appropriate, to communicate those thoughts to the leadership of the church. For such work the basic question would be:

What do we consider would best help forward the development in this church of generous Christian giving in and through the life of the church?

Chapter 9: 'Re-working evangelism'

A church, or church leadership, wanting to think through and re-shape its whole practice of evangelism would find the Emmaus introduction booklet a good basis, irrespective of whether they plan to use the Emmaus course material, or not. They would also benefit from assessing the current practice of evangelism against the following checklist (p. 190) of the marks of a 'Thorough initiation' (5) process.

Chapter 10: 'Re-working mission'

There are three further pieces which have proved of value for leaders.

'Discerning church vocation' (6) is a summary of a 16-page booklet produced originally for Sheffield diocese to help churches engage with their local community.

'The pastoral cycle' (7) is an extract from Laurie Green, *Let's Do Theology*, that explains, and earths in a specific story, how the pastoral cycle works. This is as valuable a skill for leaders to develop as Yaconelli's 'Liturgy of discernment'. They are complementary to each other.

'Making the most of MAPs' (8) is a list of ten marks of a healthy MAP and MAP process. A useful checklist for any church starting out to develop a Mission Action Plan, or engaging in the process of reviewing one already in existence.

1 Leading worship

Discern the (open) theme

The readings, sermon subject and season of the year (lectionary) are all obvious starting points for identifying an overarching theme for an act of worship. Hymns and other musical elements then need to be chosen to carry the theme forward which is best sustained by the briefest of introductions. By *open* theme is meant one that opens up a wide area to be explored that applies to every worshipper (a prairie, e.g. *serving God*), rather than one that constricts reflection and worship or locks people out (a paddock, e.g. *witness at work*).

Be sparing with your words

In worship people are seeking to give themselves in love and attention to God. Words from the front can easily break their train of meditation, rather than move them forward. It is best to let the liturgy, scriptures and hymns/songs carry people forward. However, a word from the leader can often help.

Words said on behalf of the congregation *to* God are of more value than words said *to* the congregation about God/worship. So, rather than introducing the Collect by saying, 'The Collect for the nineteenth Sunday after Trinity' (information), say: 'That we may love God with all our heart, we pray …', thus keeping the focus on God.

Included in watching our words is the work of checking the words and sentiments of songs and hymns. Some contemporary songs focus more on our feelings than on God.

Give clear 'stage directions'

In particular, page numbers first, and directions ('Let us stand/pray/be still, etc.') last. So: 'Page x, we express our conviction about how God … in the words of the Creed – let us stand.' This gets people to the right page first, but only tells them to do something at the moment they need to.

Be alive to moments of encounter

Watch out for any sense of the presence of God and create/leave space, rather than rush on to the next part of the service. Seize such moments saying something like: 'Let's be still before God and welcome his presence [or offer ourselves afresh, to Him]'. Another way of doing this is to *give space and peace*. People live frantic, over-stimulated, lives and come to church to be part of God's reflective people. Give them the chance and help them to do so.

Let the liturgy do its work

'Liturgy' means literally 'the work of the people', or even 'public works'. People come with a desire/intention to worship, and the liturgy gives a framework and secure structure in which to do that. Material intended to substitute or supplement the liturgy often simply obscures it. Let it do its own work.

See preaching as an aid to worship and encounter

Preaching is an engagement with scripture that serves the goal of corporate worship, rather than being a stand-alone item. Look for ways of connecting it with the whole worship.

Come having worshipped this way

Worship is, in many respects, a led meditation. The leader's best preparation is to use the order of service as a framework for their own prayer, meditation and worship, noting any insights to help guide people's meditation. Then lead it as an act of worship with which you are familiar.

2 Preaching is ...

■ **a spiritual ministry.** It is exercised within an act of worship and needs to assist the encounter with God which is the heart of true worship. While containing 'information', it is much more about 'formation' and 'transformation' into Christlikeness. The energizing power of preaching is the word of God. The goal is to help people engage with God through the scriptures.

■ **an incarnate ministry.** Truth is embodied in the preacher. People are enabled to engage with God's truth because it comes through the filter of a human being/life. So the word has to grab and affect us if it is to stand a chance of doing so with others. We may be focused on 'shaping the sermon', but we need to remember that God's focus is on 'shaping the preacher' so that the word will be embodied. The issue is not how far we have grasped the scriptures, but how far God has got hold of us through them.

■ **a priestly ministry.** The priest is called to make connections between people and God. This involves making connections also between faith and life, the word and the world, and – in the context of worship – between word and sacrament. To preach is to provoke dialogue between people's faith and their experience of life.

Some lessons from experience

Let the scriptures do the shaping

Be open to the surprises, challenges and disturbing presence of what God has to say, which might be different from what we had thought the passage says. *Exegesis*, not *eisegesis*: what comes out of the passage rather than any meaning we impose upon it by our assumptions and pigeon-holing of our theology.

Identify the dominant theme

Sometimes there are several 'lines of enquiry'. At some point we have to identify which is the one we are called to address. Until we have identified this dominant theme and can encapsulate it in a word, phrase, or – at the most – sentence, we have not yet grasped 'the message'.

Let the scriptures speak to you

Otherwise it will not speak to others. See yourself as the one the passage addresses first. 'But which of them has stood in the council of the Lord to see or to hear his word? Who has listened and heard his word?' (Jeremiah 23.18).

Ask the tough questions of the passage

Jacob wrestling with the angel ('I will not let you go unless you bless me', Genesis 32.26) is the role model for sermon preparation. Arguing with the scriptures is often the key to unlocking the passage. It is not disrespectful, but an honest quest.

Let it ferment in you

Prepare as far ahead as possible so that you are mulling it over, reading commentaries, reflecting on your experience of life in the process. As Jesus said: 'The old wine is better'!

Write what you *say* rather than *read* what you *write*

After doing the hard work of preparation, I go for a walk. I then imagine telling someone what the passage says to me. This way, I only recall what has really grabbed me, and I formulate the sermon in the *spoken* rather than *written* form. That helps considerably in the sense of dialogue. A sermon is a speech, not an essay.

Proceed to checkout

We need to ask two questions 'from the congregation':

■ *So what?* What should I do/think/be in the light of what has been said?

■ *But how?* Give me some clues about specific actions I can/should take.

3 Pastoral care principles

This material is suitable for personal and group study, but is primarily designed as a checklist for those involved in the work of pastoral care to work through and apply to their own personal growth and to their work in helping others grow in the likeness of Christ. Note the questions at the end of the material, which can be used for each section.

Mutual learning

Secular pastoral work is essentially built on the expert (doctor, counsellor, etc.) delivering expertise to the (ignorant) 'laity'. All too easily it creates a passive and dependent clientele.

In contrast, Christian pastoral care is based on kneeling together before God with the same attitude. D. T. Niles, the Indian theologian, expressed evangelism as 'one beggar telling another beggar where to find bread'. This is why the right place to start in growing a new pastoral culture is with a group of people committed to practising what they are talking about and hoping to pass on to others. 'Wounded healers heal because they, to some degree at least, have entered the depths of their own experiences of loss and in those depths found hope again.'[1] This is about being willing to grow as a follower of Christ, and – for the good of others – being willing to let the marks of Christian pastoral care be authenticated first in our own lives. Some of these marks are noted below. However, they are offered not as a definitive list but more as a 'starter for ten' with the expectation that any group working on these things will want to add other elements lacking in the list, or come to the conclusion that what is listed here can be better expressed in different words.

Listening[2]

Listening is essentially an attitude to life. It includes listening to God through our whole experience of life – 'every experience is a kind of annunciation'.[3] This includes doing so through nature, art, conversations and human creativity. In a foundational way it involves listening to God through *scripture*[4] and in *prayer*. Learning to listen to ourselves is another aspect of becoming a good listener. Indeed, listening, rather than giving advice, is the primary task of the pastor; for the pastor's role is to create a climate in which another person can listen to theirself and to God and discern their own chosen response. The primary task is to facilitate people's encounter with God, not to tell them what to do.

Holiness above happiness

The goal of pastoral care is to help other people become holy, godly people. It is not always, or primarily, about making others happy (or even about them liking us). We need to be open to how God's call to *us* is moving us on. *What is my next step into a greater likeness to Christ?* Again, the three dimensions of our knowledge of God (*Up* to God in personal devotion, *In* to one another through paying loving attention, *Out* to the coming of God's kingdom in the world around us) provide us with a map of where we are being called to move on in holiness ourselves. We cannot ask others to address these questions unless we are doing so for ourselves.

Character above circumstances

All too often, when we pray for others in testing circumstances, we pray for an easing of their *circumstances*. When we look at the prayers of Paul he prays for faithfulness of character in testing circumstances more than he prays for the removal of those circumstances. What is God seeking to develop in me through the testing things I experience? Seven times Paul asks for prayer while he is in prison. What he asks for is not change of circumstances (release from prison) but courage to be faithful to Christ (release from fear).

God in our testings

The Spirit led Christ into the wilderness: so too God comes not only to comfort but also to test and refine us. He often does so by taking us through painful experiences. The Psalms can be seen as outlining this process in three stages: namely:

1   *Celebrating God's ordering of the world and our lives* (Psalms of orientation[5]). We can celebrate the wonder of the world God has established and our part in it. Involved in this is both the receiving and giving of personal affirmation. Faith makes sense of life.

2   *Addressing the way God disrupts our lives* (Psalms of disorientation). God disturbs and shakes our settled order and circumstances. As Thomas Merton puts it,[6] 'In order to be true to God and to ourselves we must break with the familiar, established and secure norms and go off into the unknown.' We need to discern God's presence in our times of testing, grief, puzzlement and plain disaster. Faith provides an anchor in the storm.

3   *Connecting with how God brings us to a new beginning* (Psalms of
     re-orientation). Such psalms express the ways in which God brings
     us through testing times into a new and richer perspective on life.
     Allowing God to take us through this process prepares us to be
     alongside others in their disorientation. Faith opens up new territory
     for us to enter, explore and grow in.

In working through this material it would be good to consider the following
questions:

**Where have I experienced and seen the value of these aspects of
pastoral care?**

**What can we do to strengthen the expression of these elements of
pastoral care among us?**

4 Structures for Christian giving

Chapter 8 sought to establish the distinctive nature of Christian giving. What follows is a structure for establishing those distinctive marks in the giving of the church. Though set out as one specific plan, there are plenty of creative ways in which churches can adapt and re-work the pattern to fit local circumstances. However, care needs to be taken to avoid watering down the approach and lapsing back into a 'fundraising' rather that 'sacrificial giving' mindset and practice.

This material is probably of most use to a PCC or finance team, yet the response of church members to such an approach should be welcomed and help in the process of establishing any new developments in the handling of giving in the church.

1 Annual 'Pledge Sunday'

Each year, one Sunday to be designated as a 'Pledge Sunday'. Clearly it is important to hold such a day when most of the congregation are likely to be around. This means avoiding holiday seasons. Late November has the advantage of focusing people's minds on how they will give in the coming year. Late March puts the focus on giving in the new tax year; however, it has the disadvantage of taking place at a time that may clash with Easter and have to be moved. Each church needs to work out the most suitable time in its own calendar. They also need to decide what to call such a day. They have been called variously 'Giving to God Sunday', 'Commitment Sunday', 'Pledge Sunday' and 'Thanksgiving Sunday'.

The advantage of an annual day is that each year people are invited to think about giving for the coming year. When such occasions are held less frequently, the commitment is for a longer period and people become cautious about promising for a period in which they cannot predict their circumstances. An annual renewal and revision of financial commitment allows for changed financial circumstances to be taken into account.

2 Three-year cycle

With an annual Pledge Day there are advantages in working on a three-year cycle, with a heightened focus every third year. Suggested specifics are given below, subject, obviously, to local adaptation and variation.

In normal years

- **Preaching** about giving would be given on the Sunday before the Pledge Day. Preaching on the day is too late, if people are to think about their giving before the day. Preaching on the day is much more appropriately focused on looking back with thanksgiving or looking forward with a sense of vision and vocation.

- **Information packs** should be assembled and sent to every regular worshipper three or four weeks before the Pledge Day. These packs should include

  - Brief *vision summary sheet* of current priorities for the church, and/or

  - A *letter from the incumbent* setting out the issues, priorities and financial challenges before the church.

  - A straightforward outline of the *present financial challenges* arising from those priorities and other issues and commitments.

  - A *pledge card* on which the person would state how much they planned to give, per week, per month or annually, over the next year.

  - An *envelope* in which to put, and seal, the pledge card.

  - *An invitation to all* (in such packs) to *pray*, give careful *consideration*, *decide* what they are going to do about giving for the coming 12 months, *complete* the pledge card, and *bring* it to church on the Pledge Sunday (or the nearest Sunday afterwards if they are not able to be in church on that Sunday).[7]

- **Act of giving:** in the Services on the Pledge Day, people are invited to bring their pledges forward in silence and put them on an offering plate (held by a churchwarden). People are encouraged, during this act, to offer themselves and the life of the church to God in prayer.

- **Celebration:** one reason why 'giving' should not be the subject of the preaching on the Pledge Day is that the emphasis should be on celebration and a sense of festival – a high point in the life of the church. 'Thanksgiving Day' is an appropriate title, preferably with a focus on God's giving to us.

- **Newcomers:** while it is not right to rush or pressurize newcomers to the church (or to the faith) to contribute financially, it is wise to have some form of the above packs available throughout the year so that newcomers who want to become involved in the giving can do so at any point in the year.

Every third year

- **Preaching:** on the subject of giving to take place for *three or four* Sundays prior to the Pledge Day. Having a visiting preacher on the Pledge Day (but again, not preaching about giving) can help to make this a special day.

- **Visiting:** some strategy be developed to visit people in their homes to deliver the information packs, to explore issues with people and listen to their experiences (both of blessing and struggle in the area of giving). It may not be right or possible to visit every church member every three years but it is certainly good to visit all those who have joined the church since the start of the previous three-year cycle. Such visiting can fruitfully be done by PCC members, suitably trained, who would also use such visits as a consultation process with church members about the direction and priorities of the church. If this is done, it is best done in the month before the Pledge Day, with their visiting replacing the PCC meeting for that month.

- **Home groups:** where such exist in a church, it is good to provide them with study material so that they can engage with the subject together.

3 Pledge forms

Careful thought needs to be given to these forms.

- They need to be **well produced**, clear and as simple as possible.

- They need to **maximize choice** about how people give. For example, people should be given the option to say how much they will give per *week*, per *month*, or per *year*, since different people think in different time-frames about their finances. Couples should be allowed to give as a couple or as two individuals – according to their choice.

- **Gift Aid giving** should be commended and the option made easily available.

- **Confidentially assured:** It is important that giving is anonymous and that people are informed of this. Having a person's name/address on one side and the details of their giving on the other is a way of achieving this.

- **Everyone to complete one:** it is best to invite everyone to complete a pledge card, even where they are not changing the level of their giving. This enables the giver to make a new commitment to sustain their giving and participate in the act of giving. It enables the church to know its assured income.

The whole process, at every stage, needs to maintain a primarily visionary, spiritual exercise dynamic, rather than become a purely administrative or financial function.

5 Thorough initiation checklist[8]

The early Church (first four centuries) did a very thorough job of initiation. This is the term used to describe the whole process of bringing people to faith and enabling them to be 'changed into the likeness of Christ'. It is a much richer view of the work of initiation than that of getting people to 'pray the sinner's prayer' or 'make a decision for Christ'. We might not want to use those words today, but we should not abandon seeking to help people at the 'crossover point'. What we do need to do is to see such work is part of a bigger whole, a whole that involves the whole Church and the whole gospel.

One way of grasping that wholeness of the gospel is to see that what needs to be passed on to others functions at three levels. First, we need to impart *information*, particularly in an age where people have lost the cultural rooting in the faith. Second, a process of *formation* needs to take place through which our lives, and especially what we do (our behaviour) comes to reflect the truth we see and the faith we hold. Third is a process of *transformation* through which our character (who we are) comes to reflect something of the likeness of Christ and the image of God.

These three stages will include changes at various levels and over various time-frames. They do not happen neatly at conversion. Some will have begun before, and all of them will be elements into which we are called to grow throughout our lives. The Christian is rightly called a disciple; this means a learner. That process lasts a lifetime. It will involve our hearing and responding to God's call to grow in the following.

Spirituality

How we relate to God, including our personal prayer and meditation, our discerning God's call on our lives and our part in the spiritual life of the community of faith. Newcomers need help in getting established in good, but achievable, disciplines in this fundamental area of faith. These are the 'Up', 'In', 'Out' modes that this book is about.

Self-acceptance

The fact that Christians practise repentance does not mean we should always be putting ourselves down. Rather, true repentance leads us into the joy of being forgiven people who know they are loved and accepted by God even when they fail. Christian maturity is about being honest about our gifts and our blind-spots and putting both at the disposal of God for him to take, use and redeem.

Character

Our prayers betray our concern that God will change our circumstances.
In his mercy God does often act to help there, but God's first priority is
to change our character, conforming us more fully to the true humanity
to which he is calling us. This change can come about through testing
circumstances that draw out the response of greater maturity and grace.
God is working on who we are, not just what we do.

Community

Belonging is one of the great fruits of believing; just as it is often the
experience that leads to faith. Either way, because God, the Three-in-One,
is community, following him leads us into community that is diverse,
gifted and yet able to become harmonious. Like an orchestra, each has a
part to play, but it is the whole that makes music for God and for others as
a community lives out the divine command to love God and to love others.
Where that is not happening, our call is to play our part in helping to bring
that about – by the grace of God.

Worldview

Our nurture and the surrounding culture give us a way of seeing the world
– getting on, getting things, getting recognition, being some of them.
The gospel introduces us to a very different understanding of the world.
Created by God and populated by people made in his image (though
marred as well), God is at work to bring all people and all creation to its
intended fulfilment of its nature. Wonder, seeing the sacred nature of life
and the beauty of so much, draws out from the believer a response to this
world that is full of thankfulness, compassion, enjoyment and passion for
justice, mercy and understanding between peoples.

Lifestyle

This is about how we handle the practicalities of living, and reveals what
we really consider important enough to influence our decisions. This
affects deeply our attitude to ourselves, to other people, to material
possessions, and reflects our motivation and our priorities. The message
of Christ needs to be expressed in the lifestyle we adopt – or are we living
by inherited values or influenced by the surrounding cultural values that go
against the call of God in Christ?

Mission/vocation

This is about the call of all who name the name of Christ to be caught up in God's loving purposes for all creation. When we see initiation as being into the kingdom of God rather than just the Church, it then goes to the heart of who we are and what we are about. The true test of effective initiation is not so much what sort of church members it produces, as what sorts of whole human beings emerge from the process.

Where do these elements connect with our experience?

What are the implications of these elements for how we set about helping others on the journey to faith and the journey of faith?

6 Discerning church vocation

'Discerning Church Vocation' is the structure and booklet produced for the Sheffield diocese to help them listen to their local communities.[9] In summary the pattern is as follows.

Personal, rather than written, invitations to be given to key people in the community to give 90 minutes in a month or two's time to help the church reflect on the needs of the local community and how it can best fulfil its role in the community.

As wide a spread of people as possible (e.g. not *all* professional carers, let's have some community characters, etc.), including age range. If inviting some sixth-formers it is best to invite two or three, not one on their own.

Hold the meeting *off* church premises. Make sure there is a reasonable PCC representation so more than the vicar are hearing what is being said, but brief them beforehand to come to listen and to ask questions, rather than give answers, or talk much.

After the welcome, ask three people, previously invited and briefed about length of input, etc., to share three characteristics or concerns about their community.

Possibly get people in small buzz-groups to share response and then get groups to share any thoughts they have had with the wider group. Avoid too ponderous a process. Not every group needs to report back, and keep it to a reasonable time length. Here the goal is to identify the two or three key issues that have emerged. Gather any ideas about what needs to be done about them. Also gather information about the way in which anyone is working on these areas already.

Then move the group on to talk about what role they see the church playing in all this. Make sure any small groups working on this have a PCC member with them, thus ensuring that everything that is said will have been heard by a PCC member.

Conclude with thanks to all who have participated and promise to send something in writing to them within six months to tell them what has emerged out of this meeting.

The church (PCC members) need to report back to the PCC, and some process should be developed to ensure that action is taken to address at least one element of what has emerged. Get into action and report back to the original group.

You might want to re-convene a similar group in a year or two's time.

Remember: thorough preparation is the key to this approach working well.

7 The 'pastoral cycle'

At the heart of the re-working of the church's engagement in mission and evangelism we need to find a way in which spirituality, the coming of the kingdom, integrity and self-giving love can come together. One valuable aid to achieving that is through the use of what is called the 'pastoral cycle', though it might better be described as the 'mission cycle'. It is a simple framework for reflecting, from a theological rather than secular perspective, on what we are doing in any mission venture. This 'mission model' is equally valuable as an 'evangelism model'.

This comes originally from the Church in South Africa where it was expressed in the three-stage process as see–judge–act. In the process the *seeing* is about taking time to reflect on the situation we are engaged with and what action we discern as being needed. The *judging* is about reflecting theologically on what we are doing and what is going on. The final stage, of *acting*, is when we *see* what is happening, *judge* what God is doing, and then *act* on the call of God to us in the situation.

Bishop Laurie Green has, over many years, developed this in the British context in his book *Let's Do Theology*.[10] His framework is as follows:

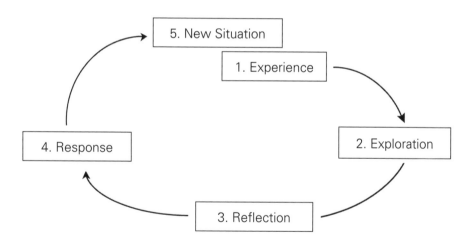

How this process works is best described in one of his stories. It is of the re-vitalizing of an ageing and declining women's knitting circle. If some process can bring that sort of group to life, surely there is hope for us all!

A small group of elderly women had been meeting together for some years to knit for the Leprosy Mission. Over the course of time their numbers had dwindled, but faithful members still met once a week to share a cup of tea, to knit and to raise money for the charity.

The process began with their *experience*.[11] The women spoke first of the sheer enjoyment of producing a knitted garment, second of the companionship engendered by their meetings, and third of their sense of concern for lepers.

Then, after sharing these feelings, we moved on to more detailed *exploration*. We looked analytically at the mechanism of knitting, in which a long woollen thread is manipulated by means of needles into complex patterns and garments, which offer durability, warmth and beauty. Then, after exploring this process of creativity, we moved on to consider the composition of the group itself and began to appreciate the variety that was represented there. Third, we explored the issue of leprosy, and shared a slide presentation all about the subject.

Having thus explored, we moved round the cycle to *reflection*. The first of our reflections was related to the process of creation in which the knitters had been involved. As they read the stories of creation they felt more appreciative of the joy that God must have felt during the creation, for they themselves had had a glimpse of that joy even in their own small attempts at creativity. From there, they moved on to concern themselves with the make-up of their group and reflected on the diversity within it. This diversity, they felt, had produced a much more interesting and buoyant group and they recognized the extent to which they relied on the variety of gifts that such diversity offered. They felt that this mutual reliance upon the creative gits of others in the group mirrored what St Paul had written about the Church. Each spiritual gift was important, he said, for each was the distinctive offering that a member makes to the whole body (1 Corinthians 12). This interrelatedness of each member and each gift with the next became a central feature of the group's thinking. If just one stitch in the knitted garment should be dropped, then the whole garment would be at risk of becoming undone.

When they finally turned their attention to those who suffer leprosy, they were soon able to make the connection between what they had so far learnt and the fact that Jesus had taken especial trouble to reach out to those whose bodies had been spoilt and marred by disease – where the creation had come to grief – and he had bound those lepers back into the body of society; no longer outcast, but precious, and once again integrated into human society. The dropped stitch had been reworked into the garment.

How pertinent the connection was between the group's creative knitting of single stitches into whole, complete garments and the healing and inclusion into society of those who had experienced the separation and disintegration that leprosy wrought.

It was this reflection that prompted the little group to move on to *response*, to further committed action. They decided that they would try to enlarge their knitting circle and offer membership to those who, like the lepers, were usually barred from society. They sought out the housebound and frail and visited them regularly in order to sit and knit with them where that was possible. They also brought their learning to the attention of other Christians by setting up a display stall in the church entrance hall. They took responsibility for a service of worship where hymns and readings told stories of creation, of lepers being healed and society finding new wholeness and completeness. And finally, they found their group growing, not only numerically, but, from having been a rather lack-lustre gathering, they were now a vibrant and inspired group determined to continue the search and make their contribution towards a better society.

That telling story reminds us what it means to return to the heart of our faith and church life and to re-work the church's life around its relationship to God, one another and the world around us. If such steps can renew the life of an ageing knitting group, what might it do for the life of a whole church?

8 Making the most of Mission Action Plans

Mission Action Plans are being used increasingly by churches in the UK and this section is designed to help churches get off to a good start by making the most of investing time in developing such a plan.

MAPs resourcing, www.churchmaps.co.uk, is a helpful source of information about what dioceses are doing and learning from the MAP-making process. Worth visiting.

The four stages of the MAP process:

1   **Planning:** the vital groundwork of prayerful and wide consultation needed to develop a good MAP. An important part of this is the work of listening – to God, the Church and the wider community.

2   **Implementing:** the real work of a MAP is doing what we have identified as God's call on his Church.

3   **Reviewing:** whether working on a one-year or five-year perspective, an annual review is an essential element.

4   **Revising:** revising our original plans in light of experience.

Ten marks of healthy MAPs

1   **Rooted in prayerful reflection**. Good MAPs are the result of discerning what God is wanting to do with us rather than what we are going to do for God. *Question*: 'How do you make God laugh?' *Answer*: 'Tell him your plans!' Prayerful discernment of the church's vocation is what our MAP needs to articulate.

2   **Wide consultative process.** Rightly understood, a church's vision and vocation arise out of the faith community rather than things to be imposed upon it, though in some situations a 'starter for ten' from the leadership, may be needed to get things going. People today are much more likely to put their energies into plans they have been involved in shaping than into plans imposed on them without consultation. Moreover, they are the most likely source of 'ideas that work'.

Ideally this should extend to the local community and to seeking their views of what is needed and how the church might best serve the area. However, this should be seen as valuable listening, rather than necessarily defining the call of God on the church.

3   **Good grasp of present church state.** We cannot undertake a journey unless we know our starting point. Some options here are:

- Updating the Parish Profile.
- SWOT analysis (**S**trengths, **W**eaknesses, **O**pportunities, **T**hreats), or using in-depth surveys.
- *The Healthy Churches' Handbook* (Robert Warren, CHP, 2004).
- *Natural Church Development* (Christian Schwarz).

4   **Rooted in spirituality/theology/vocation.** Good MAPs are energized by a sense of call from God arising from an awareness of his loving purposes in the world.

> Many parish churches overwhelm themselves with actions, meetings and projects that are not necessarily directed by careful theological reflection, and may in fact be a squandering of their energies and resources rather than a faithful commitment to engage incarnationally with God in the world.[12]

5   **Clear sense of direction for next five years**. Anglican churches are familiar with the Quinquennial Survey of Church Buildings. MAPs can helpfully be seen as *a quinquennial survey of the church's life and mission.* This gives a longer-term framework than churches often work with ('Most people overestimate what they can achieve in one year and underestimate what they can achieve in five years'). If that time-frame is used, it is vital to build in an *annual review* (see 10 below).

6   **Sharp priorities widely communicated.** A MAP is more than a list of everything a church can, or 'ought', to do. MAPs are not a way of overburdening ourselves, but focusing action, enabling churches to work 'smarter rather than harder'.

7   **Healthy balance between doing and being.** The danger of activism needs to be addressed ('Before we can be a mission-shaped Church, we have to be a God-shaped people'[13]). A useful framework here is to consider:

- *Looking up:* how, corporately and individually, do we need to develop our relationship with God which is the energy source for all healthy mission?
- *Looking in:* we are called to incarnate the truth, not just preach it. How can the way the church operates, and handles internal relationships, demonstrate the Good News of God incarnate in the life of a community for the sake of the world?

- *Looking out:* how are we called, and gifted, to serve the needs of others in the local community and the wider world – remembering that most church members engage with others on a much wider span than just 'the parish'?

8   **Specific achievable actions.** Many dioceses using MAPs encourage the making of SMART plans; that is, plans that are **S**pecific and **S**tretching, **M**easurable, **A**chievable, **R**elevant and **R**ealistic, **T**imebound.

9   **Workable plans for implementation**

Plans need to be 'well costed' about

- Who will do what?
- With whom?
- With what resources?
- Accountable to whom?

This may well require that such people are released from existing commitments in the life of the church. Some current work may have to be delayed or stopped.

10   **Identifiable plans for monitoring progress.** It is all too easy for churches to put a great deal of work into *writing* a MAP and not fully grasp that the goal is to *implement* it. Inevitably we learn from putting things into action. We learn where the gifts are, what the obstacles within the life of the church and the wider world are, and will often see that our original goal needs to be revised in the light of that experience. Building in, right from the start, regular monitoring (e.g. once a year) is essential for this to happen in order to:

- *identify and celebrate* what has been achieved;
- *honestly address* where things have not worked and/or obstacles have been encountered;
- *revise plans* in the light of that experience.

The purpose of the church is to manifest an alternative way of seeing and living life.[14]

Notes

Chapter 1

1 *Epistle to Diognetus*, quoted from James Stevenson and W. H. C. Frend, *A New Eusebius*, SPCK, 1987.

2 While the national average age is 48, the average age of church members is 61.

3 John Baillie, *Our Knowledge of God*, Oxford University Press, 1939. Sadly my copy is stamped on the fly leaf with the words 'Sheffield Polytechnic discarded'!

4 Albert Einstein, 'The World As I See It', in *Living Philosophies*, Simon & Schuster, 1931, pp. 3–7.

5 Alan Smith, *God-Shaped Mission*, Canterbury Press, 2008, p. 189.

6 The three main dynamics of Christian living are: worship and prayer; living and learning in community and speech; and action and suffering for justice, freedom, peace, goodness and truth. David Ford, *Self and Salvation*, Cambridge University Press, 1999, p. 5.

7 'The purpose of the church is to manifest an alternative way of seeing and living life.' John Westerhoff III, *Living the Faith Community*, Seabury Classics, 2004, p. 72.

8 'The church must be the first sign of what it preaches.' Michael Crosby, House of Disciples.

9 'The church's sole purpose for being is to begin living now the way the world is called to live ultimately, and to represent the promise of another reality that holds hope for the human future.' Walter Wink, *Engaging the Powers*, Fortress Press, 1992, p. 164.

10 See Charles Norris Cochrane, *Christianity and Classical Culture: A Study of Thought and Action from Augustus to Augustine*, Oxford Press, 1940.

11 See Alan Kreider, *Worship and Evangelism in Pre-Christendom*, The Alcuin Club and Grove Books Joint Study, 1995, pp. 36–9. See also, Rodney Stark, *The Rise of Christianity*, HarperOne, 1997, especially Chapter 4, 'Epidemics, Networks and Conversion'.

12 Robert Warren, *The Healthy Churches' Handbook*, Church House Publishing, 2004.

13 Robert Warren, *Being Human, Being Church,* Marshall Pickering, 1995; 2nd edition, Openbook, 2007.

14 In David Runcorn, *The Road to Growth Less Travelled*, Grove Books, 2008.

15 I use a round candle that symbolizes the world, whether 'my world', the 'church world', or the 'whole created world'. Equally, other things – a cross, an icon, a shell or stone – can be a visual focus and sign to us of the goodness, creativity and presence of God, which is the purpose of the candle.

Chapter 2

1 Matthew Fox, *Creation Spirituality: Liberating Gifts for the Peoples of the Earth*, HarperSanFrancisco, 1991, p. 74.
2 David Runcorn, *Spirituality Workbook*, SPCK, 2006.
3 Warren, *The Healthy Churches' Handbook*, pp. 44–6.
4 For example, any (or preferably, over an extended period, all) of the four books recommended in the Resources section on Mission can really re-shape a group's, and church's, view of what we can do.
5 See Stephen Cottrell, *Do Nothing to Change Your Life*, Church House Publishing, 2009.
6 This is explored more fully in Chapter 10.
7 See the Leaders' Resources section, 'Making the Most of MAPs' on page 202.
8 Runcorn, *The Road to Growth Less Travelled*, p. 3.
9 Michael Fullan, *Change Forces*, The Falmer Press, 1993, p. 49.
10 Warren, *The Healthy Churches' Handbook*, pp. 91–101 and 133–40.
11 See further on this subject in Chapter 7.
12 See the next section, 'Losing sight of God's agenda'.
13 Warren, *The Healthy Churches' Handbook*, pp. 26–31.
14 Mark Yaconelli, *Contemplative Youth Ministry*, SPCK, 2006; see Chapter 10, 'The Liturgy of Discernment', for a fuller description of this.
15 In Runcorn, *The Road to Growth Less Travelled*, pp. 23–4.
16 If a group, such as the PCC, is not used to working in small or buzz groups, or used to praying extempore prayer together, then this needs to be done in simple stages. This approach might work well, in full, on a PCC awayday, but not in normal meetings. Simple steps need to be taken to get people used to such practices. So, for example, if there is a major issue or a report that has been presented, getting people to talk in groups of three and to identify an issue it raises can be helpful. With one-sentence feedback from each group, it need take only ten minutes. As far as prayer is concerned, the PCC could be invited to pray for those who exercise leadership in the church. After an opening prayer or time of silence, people could be asked to name those they want to pray for and the area of leadership they are involved in. These are simple steps on the way to getting the PCC to practise this liturgy of discernment in full.

Chapter 3

1 G. K. Chesterton, *Everlasting Man*, Hodder & Stoughton, 1925.
2 Peter Rollins, *How (Not) to Speak of God*, SPCK, 2006, p. 64.
3 Re-worked for today's culture, for example, through Taizé and in the writings of Abbot Christopher Jamieson of Worth Abbey.
4 A profound work from the evangelical tradition that has been one of the most influential books (all 435 pages) in my own spiritual journey is Richard Lovelace, *Dynamics of Spiritual Life*, InterVarsity Press, 1980.
5 Rollins, *How (Not) to Speak of God*, p. 64.
6 Wonderfully documented in the great work by J. Wesley Bready, *England: Before and After Wesley*, Hodder & Stoughton, 1939.
7 See Ann Morisy, *Journeying Out*, Morehouse, 2004, and her insightful comments about *apt liturgy* (pp. 156–64).
8 See Lynda Barley, *Christian Roots, Contemporary Spirituality*, Church House Publishing, 2006, pp. 47–9.
9 See Marva Dawn, *Reaching Out Without Dumbing Down*, Eerdmans, 1995.
10 Runcorn, *The Road to Growth Less Travelled.*
11 Roberta Bondi, *To Pray and To Love*, Burns and Oates, 1991, p. 107.
12 James Philip, *Christian Maturity*, IVF, 1964, who goes on to say: 'The greatest saints of God have been characterized, not by haloes and an atmosphere of distant unapproachability, but by their humanity. They have been intensely human and lovable people with a twinkle in their eyes.'
13 *The Times*, Wednesday 18 January 2012.
14 See Chapters 5 and 6; see also the principle of obliquity spelt out by Ann Morisy in *Journeying Out*, pp. 11ff.
15 John Holmes, *When I Am Weak*, Daybreak, 1992. This, together with his Grove Book, *Vulnerable Evangelism: The Way of Jesus*, Grove, 2003, are excellent practical resources to help individuals and churches going through testing times of weakness to find God in those times.
16 Robert Warren, *Living Well*, Fount, 1998.
17 Matthew 5.3.
18 Author of *Religion in Britain Since 1945*, Wiley Blackwell, 1994, and *The Sociology of Religion*, Sage, 2007, among others.
19 A similar, but more developed and long-term story, is told by Yaconelli, *Contemplative Youth Ministry*, pp. 128–31.
20 The following material is based on David Foster, *Reading with God*, Continuum, 2005, especially pp. 1–4.
21 J. Neville Ward, *Five for Sorrow, Ten for Joy*, Church House Publishing, 2005, p. 3.

Chapter 4

1 See Rodney Stark, *The Rise of Christianity*, HarperCollins, 1996.
2 Kenneth Woodward, in *Newsweek*, reviewing Stark, *The Rise of Christianity*.
3 Stark, *The Rise of Christianity*, p. 161.
4 Paul Tournier, *To Understand Each Other*, John Knox, 1967, p. 8. 'Listen to all the conversations of our world, between nations as well as those between couples. They are for the most part dialogues of the deaf.'
5 See the booklet *Listening for Mission*, Church House Publishing, 2006.
6 Smith, *God-Shaped Mission*, pp. 145–7. See also his Chapter 12 on the allied subject of learning.
7 See the 'In practice' section on p. 48 for an actual example of this.
8 See pp. 199–201, The 'pastoral cycle', and Laurie Green, *Let's Do Theology*, Mowbray, 1990.
9 Thomas R. Kelly, *A Testament of Devotion*, HarperSanFrancisco, 1996.
10 Green, *Let's Do Theology*, p. 103.
11 Yaconelli, *Contemplative Youth Ministry*.
12 See Runcorn, *The Road to Growth Less Travelled*.
13 Both with church members, some of whom may well have particular skills in the aspect we are seeking to develop, and also with any 'experts', authors or practitioners with whom we have contact.
14 Diane R. Westmoreland, 'Can spiritual maturity be nurtured?', Durham, 2011. This D.Th.M. thesis can be viewed online at: http://etheses.dur.ac.uk/3276/.
15 The course material called 'Exploring Prayer' is in Appendix 6 of the thesis on pp. 235–47.
16 Remember the Michael Fullan quote, on p. 20: 'Changing formal structures is not the same as changing norms, habits, skills and beliefs.'
17 A similar story, about a church focused on *nurturing its prayer life*, can be found on pages 67–8.
18 Soul Spark is a six-session course that opens up some of the riches of the Christian tradition to enable a deeper and healthier spirituality. See Nick Helm, *Soul Spark: A Short Course Exploring Prayer and Spiritual Growth*, Grove Books, 2006.
19 However, it should be noted that the goal is to develop a listening church, not to do lots of activities (see 'Goals' and 'Means', in Chapter 2).
20 In Dennis Linn, Sheila Fabricant Linn and Matthew Linn, *Sleeping with Bread*, Paulist Press, 1995. This delightful book is only 73 pages long, including several full picture pages, but is, nonetheless, a serious adult book.

Chapter 5

1 Gerald Brocollo, *Vital Spiritualities*, Ave Maria Press, 1990.
2 Fox, *Creation Spirituality*.
3 J. Drane, *What is the New Age Saying to the Church?*, Marshall Pickering, 1991, p. 22.
4 Jean Pierre de Causade, *Self-abandonment to Divine Providence*, Burns & Oates, 1933.
5 'Some are so tied up in programmes of spiritual self-improvement that they have no time to care about anything but the throbbing self-concern at the centre of their consciousness.' Richard Lovelace, *Dynamics of Spiritual Life*, InterVarsity Press, 1980, p. 160.
6 'Growth in understanding God is a matter of learning to put more of ourselves into everything we are and do, thereby becoming more alive and thus participating in God's creative work.' Nicholas Lash, *Believing Three Ways in One God*, SCM Press, 2003.
7 'There is no life not lived in community and no community not lived in praise of God.' T. S. Eliot, 'Choruses from the Rock', in *Collected Poems 1909–1935*, Faber & Faber, 1958.
8 Lash, *Believing Three Ways in One God*.
9 For another framework for what could be called 'the marks of a healthy Christian spirituality', see Wesmoreland's 'Model of Maturity', at http://etheses.dur.ac.uk/3276/, pp. 95–9.
10 James Philip, *Christian Maturity*, IVP, 1964, pp. 70–1.
11 Gerard Hughes, *God of Surprises*, Darton, Longman & Todd, 1985, p. 62.
12 David Ford, *The Shape of Living*, HarperCollins, 1997, p. 35.
13 D. B. Murray, 'Implicit religion: the hospice experience', in E. Bailey (ed.), *The Secular Quest for Meaning in Life*, Edwin Mellen Press, 2002, pp. 237–50, p. 244.
14 Rollins, *How (Not) to Speak of God*, pp. 24–5.
15 See further in Chapter 7, the section 'Resourcing the leaders', p. 90.
16 Nick Helm, *Soul Spark*.
17 See also Robert Warren and Kate Bruce, *Life Source*, Church House Publishing, 2006.
18 Yaconelli, *Contemplative Youth Ministry*, p. 165.
19 Because no one was used to praying out loud, the priest began by handing out prayer topics as people came into the meeting. People were asked to pray the prayer aloud, either reading what they had been handed or expressing it in their own words, then ending 'Lord, in your mercy', for others to respond, 'Hear our prayer.'
20 Yaconelli, *Contemplative Youth Ministry*, pp. 52–3. All the words are his. I have added the paragraph breaks and the words in italics to draw out the steps in the process.

Chapter 6

1 Alastair Campbell, *Rediscovering Pastoral Care*, Darton, Longman & Todd, 2nd edition, 1986.
2 This can be helped greatly where a leaders' group, as outlined in Chapter 7, is in place.
3 See Roberta Bondi quote on p. 32.
4 See the 'Listening exercise' in the Resources Section, pp. 150–2.
5 'It took a single night to get Israel out of Egypt, but it took 40 years to get Egypt out of Israel.'
6 It has too technical and potentially authoritarian a ring. Moreover, for those from a Nonconformist background, it is associated with clergy and, maybe, clericalism.
7 John Holmes, *Challenging Questions for Churches Wanting to Grow*, Grove Books, 2009, has some helpful and practical suggestions ('Sharing the Care', pp. 18–20). Though focused particularly on larger churches, these ideas – suitably adapted – apply to most churches.
8 Here it might be worth circulating beforehand a copy of 'What is worship?' (or some adapted or alternative version) from the Resources section of this book (pp. 155–6) to serve as a discussion starter.
9 The church in the story told on p. 47 is seeking to develop its spiritual life. As part of this process it is designing a questionnaire that can be used in pastoral visits. This is a good illustration of how this 'Listening team' model might work out in practice.

Chapter 7

1 The only question asked more frequently has been, 'How can we get people to buy into the vision we have for our church?' My answer to this is, 'Get them to design the vision.' The problem is that the leadership has already designed the vision and are not keen for them to knock it about!
2 As a charismatic Catholic priest tellingly put it: 'Groups are very good at developing little rituals of dishonesty, ways of systematically evading real issues.' Simon Tugwell, *Did You Receive the Spirit?*, Darton, Longman & Todd, 1972, p. 122.
3 Chapter 2, pp. 21–2, on confusing *means* and *goals*.
4 Joseph Myers, *The Search to Belong*, Zondervan, 2003, is a stimulating contribution to this subject.
5 See Alan Jamieson, *A Churchless Faith*, SPCK, 2002, especially Chapter 8 where he maps people's movement through Fowler's 'stages of faith' and relates it to the stages of faith the church communities are at.
6 John Wesley, 'There is no such thing as solitary religion'; Dietrich Bonhoeffer, 'There is no such thing as an individual Christian'; T. S.

Eliot: 'There is no life that is not in community, and no community not
lived in praise of God.'

7   See Chapter 4.
8   See Emmaus Growth Book IV, *Your Kingdom Come*, pp. 72–7 for an
    exercise designed to help a group find a goal beyond itself. Also, *Life
    Calling*, Church House Publishing, is a five-session course designed to
    help all participants discover their *vocation* – in the whole of life – not
    just the life of the church.
9   See Walter Wink, *Transformative Bible Study*, Abingdon, 1989; and
    John Finney, *Leading an Emmaus Group*, Church House Publishing,
    2004 (about leading *any* small group and good to give to all such
    leaders).
10 See Chapter 2, pp. 24–5 and Yaconelli, *Contemplative Youth Ministry*,
    Chapter 10, 'The Liturgy of Discernment', for a fuller description of
    this, pp. 115–31.
11 http://www.lichfield.anglican.org/chadnet/DynamicContent/
    Documents/World%20Mission/Community_of_St_Chad_Leaflet.pdf.

Chapter 8

1   See Rollins, *How (Not) to Speak of God*, Chapter 5, 'The Third Mile'
    for a searching reflection on the nature of generosity in the heart of
    God's love that we are called to incarnate in our lives.
2   Yaconelli, *Contemplative Youth Ministry*, p. 44.
3   'The First Greek Life' in *Pachomian Koinonia*, Vol. 1, trans. and ed.
    Armand Veilleux, Cistercian Publications, 1980.
4   Francis Schaeffer, *True Spirituality*, Tyndale House, 1971.
5   Rollins, *How (Not) to Speak of God*, pp. 65 and 70.
6   Morisy, *Journeying Out*.
7   Which Karl Rahner suggests is at the heart of discipleship. Karl
    Rahner, *Theological Investigations XI*, Darton, Longman & Todd, 2001.
8   A theologically appropriate term. It is also an illustration of how
    the *goal* can be creatively embodied in the title of the *means* – see
    Chapter 2, p. 21.

Chapter 9

1   David Bosch, *Transforming Mission*, Orbis, 1991.
2   Rollins, *How (Not) to Speak of God*, p. 99.
3   Yaconelli, *Contemplative Youth Ministry*.
4   Janice Turner, *The Times*, Saturday 28 January 2012, p. 23.
5   Runcorn, *The Road to Growth Less Travelled*, pp. 3, 4.

Chapter 10

1 'Silo thinking' describes the way we think about church and faith, to be shaped by the approach and assumptions of the surrounding culture rather than by theological reflection, and application of our faith to particular situations. See more in Chapter 2, p. 18.
2 Morisy, *Journeying Out*, p. 25.
3 Andrew Bowden, *Ministry in the Countryside*, Continuum, 2003, p. xxviii.
4 Mark Gibbs and Ralph Morton, *God's Frozen People*, Fontana, 1964.
5 Robin Greenwood, *Practising Community*, SPCK, 1996, p. 64.
6 Bowden, *Ministry in the Countryside*, p. xxv
7 'The Lord bless you and keep you;
   The Lord make his face to shine upon you, and be gracious to you:
   The Lord lift up his countenance upon you, and give you peace.'
8 See Chapter 4.
9 A structure for doing this was developed for the Sheffield diocese, *Discerning Church Vocation*. A summary of this is set out in the Resources section on pages 197–8.
10 Indeed, this is sometimes the starting point for the development of Fresh Expressions.
11 J. Stevenson, *A New Eusebius*, SPCK, 1960.

Study questions

1 Laurie Green, *Let's Do Theology*, Mowbray, 1990, p. 103.
2 It will take only 20 minutes if the exercise is done once, with everyone taking on just one role. That would work best where there would be opportunity, at a later meeting, for the exercise to be repeated so everyone eventually does fulfil each role at least once.
3 In Revelation 4 and 5 there are five songs. The first two (4.8 and 4.11) speak of God as Creator. The second two (5.9–10 and 5.12) speak of Jesus as Redeemer. The final one (5.13) speaks of Father and Son in their glory as Creator and Redeemer. They are glorious expressions of worship in which God is the sole focus and centre. For more on these, see Robert Warren, *An Affair of the Heart*, pp. 57–70.
4 See the three texts quoted above: Psalms 51.15–17, Isaiah 58.4–12 and Micah 6.8.
5 Westminster Shorter Catechism (1648).
6 'Christian worship is the offering of the whole of life to God: it cannot be confined in one compartment of our lives.' Duncan B. Forrester, James I. H. McDonald and Gian Tellini, *Encounter with God*, T&T Clark International, 1996, p. 3.
7 Micah 6.6–8, Isaiah 58.1–14, Psalms 51.7–15

8   See Tim Sumpter, *Evangelistening: Recovering the Art of Listening in Evangelism,* Grove Books, 2011.

9   Philip Yancy, *What's So Amazing About Grace?,* Zondervan, 1997, p. 242.

10 This material is an adapted form of the *Action Focus Session* from Emmaus Growth Book IV: *Your Kingdom Come,* pp. 76–8. Leaders would benefit from reading pp. 72–5.

11 Yaconelli, *Contemplative Youth Ministry,* Chapters 11, 12, 13.

12 David Bosch, *Transforming Mission,* Orbis, 1991.

13 Bosch, *Transforming Mission.*

14 Dietrich Bonhoeffer.

15 'The First Greek Life' in *Pachomian Koinonia,* vol. 1, trans. and ed. Armand Veilleux, Cistercian Publications, 1980.

16 It is instructive to note that the Church at that time was strongly pacific such that a soldier could not be a member of the Church. Despite this, compassion reached out to these conscripts.

Leaders' resources

1   Campbell, *Rediscovering Pastoral Care,* p. 43.

2   See Chapter 4.

3   J. Neville Ward, *Five for Sorrow, Ten for Joy,* Church House Publishing, 2005, p. 3.

4   'Our specifically human existence consists precisely in our hearing the Word of God. We are what we hear from God.' Emil Brunner, *The Divine Imperative,* Lutterworth, 2003, p. 66.

5   Walter Brueggemann, *The Message of the Psalms,* Augsberg Fortress, 1984, from where these categories are drawn.

6   Thomas Merton, *Contemplative Prayer,* Darton, Longman & Todd, 1973, p. 26.

7   Note: it is best if even those who plan not to change their level of giving still fill in and bring their pledge card on the Pledge Sunday. It is an indication that they have given thought to the matter and assures the church that their giving will continue.

8   This is an abbreviated and revised form of the material in *Emmaus: The Way of Faith: Introduction,* Church House Publishing, 2003, pp. 21–7.

9   Copies, at the time of publication, obtainable from office@resource-arm.net.

10 Laurie Green, *Let's Do Theology,* Continuum, 2007. In the author's view, this book, along with Ann Morisy, *Journeying Out,* Morehouse, 2004, are the two best and most helpful books on mission practice around.

11 Highlighting of words has been added to the original text: Green, *Let's Do Theology*, pp. 36–9.
12 Green, *Let's Do Theology*, p. 103.
13 Smith, *God-shaped Mission*. Chapter 4 addresses this balance well.
14 John Westerhoff III, *Living the Faith Community*, Seabury Classics, 2004, p. 72.